The Entrepreneurial Game

Can You Win at it?

Published in the United States of North America

Published by CreateSpace, North Charleston, SC
ISBN-13: 978-1500520496
ISBN-10: 1500520497
Library of Congress Control Number: 2014915503

Also From Oswald R. Viva:

Customizing VLSI IC Update: A User's Guide to the
ASIC Design Center
Electronic Trends Publications

It's Lonely at the Top
A Practical Guide to Becoming a Better Leader of
Your Small Company
iUniverse, Inc.
ISBN-978-1-4620-4653-9
ISBN-978-1-4620-4655-3
ISBN-978-1-4620-4654-6

Fundamentals of Job Interviewing for Managers
Amazon.com
ISBN-13 978-148022960
ISBN-10 1480222968

Performance Reviews
The Bad, the Ugly…the Alternative
Amazon.com
ISBN-13:978-1496144157
ISBN-10:1496144155

Accountability in the Workplace
www.SkillBites.net

You Are the Owner, But Are You the Right CEO?
www.SkillBites.net

Create a Culture of Empowerment
www.SkillBites.net

Delegate to Succeed
www.SkillBites.net

Exit Strategy and Succession Planning
www.SkillBites.net

To the vast population of small business entrepreneurs who chose not to focus on why they could not do something, which is what most people do, but instead to focus on why they could and be great at it.

The Entrepreneurial Game

Can You Win at it?

Oswald R. Viva

Foreword by Nissen Isakov

"*Entrepreneurship is living a few years of your life like most people won't so you can spend the rest of your life like most people cant.*" *Anonymous*

Table of Contents

Foreword

Author's note: Mr. Isakov is a true and highly successful entrepreneur who achieved success without any outside investors. He started with an idea and the high drive to achieve as his only assets and reached his goals driven by his vision, dedication, hard work, and persistence.

I started a new business as a new immigrant with very little money twenty eight years ago. I look back over those years and realize that I was fortunate to beat the statistics on new business failures. When I started the business I did not even know then what I did not know – Wow, I did not even know what questions to ask!

Fortunately, my startup business grew consistently at a steady rate over the first fourteen years. I saw the potential of doubling the revenue at a much higher rate than previously. I learned how to get a business going and run a small business but I was not sure I personally had the capability of running a small to medium size business, so I sought out a peer advisory board that could help me develop the capabilities I thought I might need. I met Oswald Viva who owned and ran TAB (The Alternative Board; a business of peer advisory boards) in my area in July 2000 and I immediately joined his group. Oswald and my peer group were instrumental in helping me grow the business. Oswald was my coach and mentor during those years (until he retired in July 2011) and helped me transition from an entrepreneurial "fire fighter" to a leader that had learned to delegate and empower people, which was vital to managing a rapidly growing business.

I was recently asked: "If you knew then what you know now, what would you have done differently?" After some careful thought, I realized I probably would have been too scared to do anything! So fortunately, I did not know then what I know now. However, I do wish I had an inkling, just some small idea of what the potential risks were so I could have been a little better prepared for some of the obstacles I had to overcome, especially during those first few years. This book would have really served me well then.

I assume you picked up this book because you are either starting a business, trying to decide if you are ready to start a business or maybe you are at a turning point in your present business. Oswald Viva provides the reader with some key insider information on the type of questions one should ask oneself before venturing into becoming a business owner. It brings to light the questions one does not know enough to ask when starting out on this venture. These are usually the questions that come after the fact and are the questions one should have asked before entering into a business venture.

The book touches on many important aspects of starting and running a business including some non-tactical emotional issues that one may experience. It is a great guide to helping keep your head together, keep focused on the business while making one aware of the potential pitfalls. Oswald points out the importance of keeping a check on one's physical and mental health and the significance of keeping a dividing line between business life and family life.

Not only does the book describe the risks and rewards, but more importantly the personality traits that one needs or needs to develop when owning a business and passion and perseverance are key.

I think this book has value to the reader, not only in the beginning, when starting a business but also throughout the business lifecycle. It would be a good reference book to keep on hand. In addition, I would suggest that the reader write down the reasons why he or she started the business or the scenario that led them to start the business so they can refer to it when some of the hurdles appear insurmountable.

Nissen Isakov
President
LCR Embedded Systems, Inc.

Preface

This book intends to alert would-be entrepreneurs of the challenges they will face in the venture, but it is, by no means, intended to frighten or discourage them from it. Entrepreneurship is a commendable adventure, and achieving success in it is a rewarding experience. The exhilaration of success as a business owner negates all sacrifices made to reach the goal.

As a coach, I specialize in small and medium size businesses, helping their owners reach their goals. Consequently, all my books aim at that segment of the business community. This book is no exception; I address the entrepreneurial efforts of those who use their talent, vision and drive to start and manage a new business, usually without any or much outside investment, but with the tenacity necessary to reach their goals.

These are entrepreneurs who may be part of the baby boomer generation and have worked their way up from working-class backgrounds. Perhaps they had been working on various trades or had been employed in different fields, but decided to take a chance at a dream. They are not the high-tech, venture-backed executives; instead they are leaders of what some people may consider boring businesses.

I ignore in this book the so-called Silicon Valley entrepreneurs, young men and women who create companies on one product—predominantly software and internet based—receive outlandish amounts of cash from venture capitalists or angels and become millionaires or billionaires practically overnight. These entrepreneurs may have the traits discussed here but in general, those traits do not decide the success of the venture or of the entrepreneur. I admire them for what they do and what they offer the world, but I prefer to discuss the intrepid bootstrapper.

The demographics are changing and millennials tend to be the Silicon Valley-type of entrepreneurs, but those boring businesses are still everywhere, and for the valiant people who chose them, are the bread-and butter of entrepreneurial success. This is why this book is aimed at the small business entrepreneurs

Introduction

I am an entrepreneur. Just as AA members confess at their meetings, I confess that I am addicted to entrepreneurship…and proudly so.

I was a budding entrepreneur at thirteen when I started a business with my brother, which we kept for three years.

I was an entrepreneur at eighteen when I started another business with a friend.

I was an entrepreneur at twenty-one when, with another friend, I started a successful business that I left behind to come to the United States.

I was an entrepreneur when I left the security of a very successful and rewarding career with a large multinational corporation to start a company.

I was an entrepreneur when I left another secure job to join a new start-up.

I was an entrepreneur when I started my international consulting company.

I proceeded as a serial entrepreneur when I started a few other businesses and participated—as consultant—in several other ventures.

I was an entrepreneur when I started and ran, very successfully for many years, a business of peer-advisory boards for small-business owners.

Is this history surprising? No, it isn't. A study by Performance Systems Ltd., found that 84 percent of serial entrepreneurs began dreaming of starting a business before age twenty-five and an astounding 42 percent before the age of twelve.[1]

Is twelve too young an age to know if one wants to be an entrepreneur? Perhaps, but it depends on the environment in which the twelve-year-old is being raised. If parents are successful entrepreneurs or the child has been exposed to independent businesses, he or she may have been bitten by the entrepreneurial bug early on.

I was also an entrepreneur's coach for dozens of successful business owners. My fourteen-thousand-plus hours coaching them exposed me to all manner of entrepreneurial businesses with every kind of professional and personal issue.

I am qualified by all my experience to cover the subject within this book. As I always say, being a serial entrepreneur and being involved in so many entrepreneurial ventures, I learned the what-to-dos in a start-up, but—more importantly—I learned the what-not-to-dos. I have been very successful as a coach of business owners, and I apply my experiences here to advise would-be business owners.

Starting a business is a major undertaking that not every person is qualified or ready to attempt. As the owner of a start-up company, you take many risks, and you give up some of the things that you are accustomed to. It requires much sacrifice, perseverance, vision, hard work, and, in many cases, giving up large chunks of income.

Of course, it also has its rewards; the pride and joy of business ownership is a gift reserved for those who elect it. Nevertheless, before you decide that you want to join the entrepreneurial ranks, you must consider the pros compared to the cons. Do you have what it takes? Do you have the talent, traits, resources, risk tolerance, adaptability, and family support necessary to embark in the venture? Are you willing to give up many things and risk many others in search of your dream? Only if you can answer yes to all these questions should you consider starting a serious business.

Toby Thomas uses the analogy of a man riding a lion: "People look at him and think, 'This guy's really got it together! He is brave.' And the man riding the lion is thinking, 'How the hell did I get on a lion, and how do I keep from getting eaten?'"[2]

Are you willing and ready to mount the lion and survive?

Part I

The Entrepreneurial Game

Entrepreneurship, a Definition

According to *Wikipedia*, "**entrepreneurship** is the process of identifying and starting a new business venture and sourcing and organizing the required resources while taking both the risks and rewards associated with the venture."

Entrepreneurship may result in new organizations or revitalizing mature organizations in response to a perceived business opportunity.

From *Merriam-Webster*: "**Entrepreneur**: a person who starts a business and is willing to risk loss in order to make money. One who organizes, manages, and assumes the risks of a business or enterprise."

Startup. A new business started by an entrepreneur is referred to as a start-up company. In recent years, the term has been extended to include social and political forms of entrepreneurial activity.

A **startup company** or **start-up** is a company, partnership, or temporary organization designed to search for a repeatable and scalable business model. These companies, generally newly created, are in a phase of development and research for markets.

Chapter I – Game Rules

Entrepreneurial Adventure

Starting a business is looked at as glamorous, and its founders are considered heroes and lucky to have that experience, but it is not all cream and roses. Nobody said building a company was easy to do, but it should be clear that it can be psychologically excruciating in some circumstances, with the founders paying a heavy price if things don't go well.

We idolize successful entrepreneurs, such as Michel Dell, Mark Zuckerberg, Bill Gates, and many others, as well as less-known, small-business entrepreneurs who made it big (in varying degrees). What it is not well known is the struggle that many of them had to go through and the toll it may have taken on them before they reached the pinnacle.

In many cases, we do not know the lows of entrepreneurship because business leaders use the fake-it-until-you-make-it approach rather than admit their suffering. Many believe that letting the world know about their struggles would be seen as a weakness, and so they keep it hidden.

Also, not everyone who goes through those hard times makes it to the good side, and sadly, many suffer lasting damage from the experience, or worse. Ilya Zhitomirsky, the 22-year-old founder of Diaspora, and Jody Sherman who was 47, founder of Ecomom, are two sad examples of the ultimate price paid by entrepreneurs who cannot tolerate the stress of failed startups. Both committed suicide following the failure of their ventures.

Because the stress in entrepreneurship is a real health threat, a psychiatrist and former entrepreneur, Michael A. Freeman, is conducting research on mental health and entrepreneurship. Mr. Freeman says that the cause of these drastic events may be more than the stress of the job. He claims that the same traits that make entrepreneurs who they are, makes them susceptive to different emotional states.

The life of an entrepreneur is not easy and requires hard work and persistence to succeed. There is a high risk, and success is not guaranteed (see the small-business statistics further down). If the new venture fails, the entrepreneur can be without a job, income, and even all the money spent in the venture.

The risks do not stop there. The stress can take a toll on the health of the entrepreneur, and his or her family life can also suffer. The longer the purgatory of the failed saga, the deeper the damage can be. Trying to separate business from family life—an extremely difficult challenge in a start-up phase—can minimize the pain and the damage, but achieving this happens only rarely.

Despite the difficulty, keeping those family ties together is the best medicine for the stress caused by the ups and downs of a new business. I often say that "the business should be a part of your life apart from your life, but it should not be your entire life."

Also, the entrepreneur must not be reluctant to ask for help. Medical help if the body suffers—stress is a dangerous weapon against our physical being—even psychological help if he or she is having significant anxiety or depression. It shouldn't exclude the help that friends, colleagues, consultants, and advisors can provide. This type of help can be even more valuable than any health professional's help. (See the appendix on advisory boards later in the book).

In fact, entrepreneurs should surround themselves with people smarter and/or more experienced than they are and they should listen to other's ideas and advice. Similarly, when it comes to hiring employees, entrepreneurs should avoid the "yes-men" types and look for candidates who can challenge them (in a good way) and contribute with new ideas.

Presently there is much help in organizations set up to assist entrepreneurs and new ventures. Incubators offer office space and administrative services, as well as the opportunity to interact with other entrepreneurs and meet potential investors. Accelerators are another source of help that provide business advice, connections, and—unlike incubators—start-up investment in exchange for equity in the new venture.

Always keep in mind that most entrepreneurs go through some failures or partial failures before they achieve success. Persistence is one of the required traits for an entrepreneur, and failure cannot be part of his or her vocabulary, but paradoxically, knowing when to cut the losses has to be a key in strategic thinking. Unfortunately it is common to see business owners who lose it all in a faulty pursuit of a solution for an irremediable failure.

> **From my experience:** *A friend of mine used to say that during a painful startup phase of his now successful business "I was not smart enough to declare bankruptcy". In his case persistence won and he not only saved the business, but made it very successful.*

The other side of the coin, of course, is the happiness of making it as an entrepreneur and successful business owner. Challenges should not discourage you from the adventure; they should motivate you to conquer them to achieve your goal. Chances of success are much higher when following the directions and suggestions enumerated here. We must all remember that self-worth is much more important than net-worth.

Thomas Edison said, "Our greatest weakness lies in giving up. The most certain way to succeed is always to try just one more time." As an entrepreneur, this needs to be a rule. There are countless examples of entrepreneurs who failed (some on multiple occasions) but kept on trying until they finally succeeded.

Scary Statistics

The data shows that small businesses create most of the jobs in the United States, but a little-known fact is that start-ups and very young businesses create an average of three million new jobs each year. Even when start-ups are not included, young businesses of less than five years create two-thirds of all jobs. Start-up businesses are the drivers of job creation, which makes entrepreneurs crucial in the race to employ people.

Unfortunately the data also shows the high mortality of small businesses. Depending on which source you credit, the numbers change somewhat, but by any account, they are not encouraging. According to THE SBA, "Seven out of 10 new employer firms survive at least 2 years, half at least 5 years, a third at least 10 years, and a quarter stay in business 15 years or more." Census data reports that 69 percent of new employer establishments created in 2000 survived at least two years, and 51 percent survived five or more years.

Survival rates were similar across states and major industries. The Bureau of Labor Statistics data on establishment age show that 49 percent of establishments survive five years or more, 34 percent ten years or more, and 26 percent fifteen years or more.

In other words, if you start a new business in the United States, your chances of long-term success are less than 50 percent, so you must make sure that you have the personality, talent, and resources to embark on such an adventure.

Nevertheless, the number of small businesses in the US has increased 49 percent since 1982. This includes local stores and the explosion of "self-employed" entrepreneurs or "solopreneurs" (see later definition). There are twenty-seven million small businesses in the US; that is one for every eleven citizens.

What does all this mean? That entrepreneurs must go into the adventure knowing what is required to succeed and have the persistence to do it. Statistics should warn you of the challenges; your personality must drive you to overcome those challenges.

The government plays a key role in fomenting entrepreneurship by providing the environment in which entrepreneurs feel motivated to do their thing. This includes freeing new or prospective businesses from undue restrictions, such as overly demanding rules or onerous fees.

Personality Traits of Entrepreneurs

Just because you had this great idea for a better mousetrap doesn't mean that you have what it takes to be an entrepreneur. Entrepreneurs are a unique group of people. They not only think differently but also act differently. Your personality traits will determine if you are entrepreneurial material.

The old question, "Are leaders born or made?" can also be adapted to entrepreneurs. Are entrepreneurs born with the distinctive traits required, or do those traits develop over time through experience and teaching? Some innate traits are commonly found in entrepreneurs as the drivers of their entrepreneurial activities, but other traits are developed from the experiences lived.

Passion is a key trait that drives the entrepreneurial voyage of not only starting a business but also growing it and making it successful. Achieving success requires passion for what you do and the dedication to learn and practice management fundamentals. While passion is important, without a healthy dose of business fundamentals, passion has as much value as a dream.

When payables exceed receivables, when sales aren't there, when you feel overwhelmed by problems, or time lines are threatening you, passion alone won't help you. Your vision will drive you, but other traits are required to complete the disposition of entrepreneurs.

Vision is required to take an idea and make it a reality by building a business for it—a vision to see things and consider the possibilities before they exist, even if the world is saying, "It won't work." Entrepreneurs see opportunities where others may see problems. They are innovators looking for and implementing new ideas. They have the ability to see the future before it happens.

Creativity is another prerequisite of entrepreneurship—not only in creating products or services that the market will want but creativity in forming and running a business. Determining the best form for your business, the right markets for your products, the right partners to help you succeed, finding the right employees, how to solve problems, and many other demands of the business world require creativity.

Creativity is driven by imagination, so the imagination of an entrepreneur is a valuable asset to exercise. Albert Einstein said, "Imagination is more important than knowledge, for knowledge is limited to all we know and understand, while imagination embraces the entire world and all there ever will be to know and understand."

Self-determination and self-confidence are also required. As you create a business, you will feel lonesome even if you have partners or others you trust. You will be making all—or most—decisions, and thus, you must trust your instincts and not be afraid of making mistakes or of an occasional rejection.

As a small-business owner, you will need to negotiate everything from leases to contract terms to rates. Polished negotiation skills will help you save money and keep your business running smoothly. In your negotiations, you must be persuasive, particularly when it comes to selling your ideas, products, and services. You must also be persuasive to recruit employees and other stakeholders of the business and in dealing with other business owners.

You will need Resilience to overcome obstacles and, yes, even failures, because, chances are, there will be failures. As Sir Winston Churchill said, "A successful person is someone who can go from failure to failure with enthusiasm." A drastic failure may be too much for most people to handle, but an entrepreneur must have the ability to see failures as opportunities to learn and improve.

Ability to get things done. It is not enough to have the vision; entrepreneurs also need to have the ability to get the job done—in other words, to make goals become reality. Vision without action is a dream without end. As a business grows and the organization grows with it, people management becomes a large part of the job. This can be demoralizing because people problems are the most frustrating and painful of the headaches that businesses can offer the owner.

Entrepreneurs need to have the ability to separate the real and valuable from the noise in the overloaded world of information that exists today. Together with that, you need the ability to prioritize and focus on the really important, not just the urgent.

Communication skills are a prime trait of entrepreneurs. You need the ability to communicate one-on-one to truly connect with people, as opposed to one-to-many in sound bites through social networks. You must remember that communication is a two-way event and that listening to really hear what people have to say is a major part of the event.

Curiosity is also key. You must have the courage to ask questions that others will not and explore the details of the subject to see how you can benefit or to filter what can be damaging. Entrepreneurs are driven by the curiosity of seeing what is not there and seeking the opportunities that may be available.

You need the courage to attempt things that others will not and that, on the surface, may be risky but can yield positive results. A dose of audaciousness is a valuable ingredient to add to the recipe for entrepreneurship. To have an idea that seems a little over-the-top is OK, but it has to be real and well planned and not appear to be a gimmick.

Nothing entrepreneurial happens until the conviction of what you do raises the level of courage above the fear of failure. Courage is needed because the stakes are always high, and failure can manifest in many forms. Fear of financial losses, professional setbacks, and even personal embarrassment must be conquered with courage.

Have the tenacity to keep trying when others give up. Entrepreneurs have a high pain threshold and do not let themselves become discouraged by roadblocks encountered on the way to success.

You not only must accept risk, you must thrive on it. You must be willing to do anything to take your idea—be it a product or a service—all the way, despite obstacles that may develop along the way. Entrepreneurs take risks while knowing that, whether they succeed or fail, they will learn something useful.

Faith is necessary. Entrepreneurs and business owners

believe in themselves and in their vision and muddle through the highs and lows to reach set goals.

Gallup, the global research firm studied more than four thousand business founders to understand the driving traits and determined the ten most significant. They are:

- Risk taker
- Focus
- Determination
- Delegator
- Knowledge seeker
- Creative thinker
- Confident
- Promoter
- Independent
- Relationship builder

It is not surprising that the top trait is risk taking. Risk is the name of the game in entrepreneurship, for no new business can exist without risk. It follows too that without focus and determination, a company cannot survive and grow, and as the company grows, the founder/owner must learn to delegate.

As implied in the definition, an entrepreneur has the ambition for more. The *more* can be more information, more recognition, more money, more prestige or more "stuff", but it can also be more business-related achievements, like more productivity, more efficiency, more speed, and the respect that comes with it.

Of course, lots of people want more of something (particularly money), but an entrepreneur, because of who he or she is, has the ability to reach the goal of achieving more. The drive to achieve and the persistence to do it allow entrepreneurs to embark in the ventures that will help them reach those goals.

Do what you love and love what you do. Focus on what you can do and ignore what you cannot do.

Chapter II – Types of Players

Intrapreneurship in the Workforce

Entrepreneurs may also be found employed by large and small companies. This may sound like a contradiction, but some people have the entrepreneurial drive without the rest of the traits of true entrepreneurs, such as risk tolerance. Entrepreneurship within a firm or large organization has been referred to as intrapreneurship.

In 1992, *The American Heritage Dictionary* acknowledged the popular use of a new word, "intrapreneur," to mean "a person within a large corporation who takes direct responsibility for turning an idea into a profitable finished product through assertive risk taking and innovation." Intrapreneurship is now known as the practice of a corporate management style that integrates risk taking and innovation approaches, as well as the reward and motivational techniques that are more traditionally thought of as being the jurisdiction of entrepreneurship.

Catherine Guilford, a senior writer at Entrepreneur.com, said that it used to be that entrepreneurs were the renegade cowboys out in Silicon Valley.[3] Nowadays, you have to be an entrepreneur just to get and hold a job. Intrapreneurship can be defined as an entrepreneurial employee who takes initiative and assumes ownership of the performance of a team. Entrepreneurship doesn't happen unless someone takes ownership of execution and the results obtained, including accountability for failures.

Consultants and freelancers are cheaper than full-time staffers with benefits. Software developers overseas cost a fraction of those in the United States. And by 2030, robots will be able to perform most manual labor, according to San Francisco-based start-up organization Funders and Founders.[4] Even employees who work for large corporations are encouraged to be intrapreneurs, meaning that they are, in many cases, given company time to come up with disruptive ways of thinking about corporate organization and practices.

An employee may have an idea for a new product or process or system and he/she feels sure of its value to the business, but is afraid to expose it because he/she does not want to place the company at risk. Also, since the idea is not "within the normal scope" of his/her work there may be reluctance from management to accept it.

While external entrepreneurs consider cost, time, investment, etc. as the primary consideration in evaluating an idea, intrapreneurs are more concerned with management reaction and relationships within the organization. Peers and immediate management become the first judges of the idea and the originator of the idea may fear rejection by them.

These employed entrepreneurs can be extremely valuable to companies because they can power economic change through their vision and creative ideas. Particularly for those businesses dealing with new products or processes, the ability to identify these people can give them a marked advantage. Consequently, their employers should do what they must to retain the star performers so that they will not leave and take their new ideas with them to start a new venture.

Intrapreneurship employees must be provided with a forum free from tight corporate policies that would limit their activities to express their ideas and vision. If they feel restricted, they will become disengaged and may even resent the employer and its management. That can translate into taking their ideas to a competitor or becoming a competitor themselves.

Research by TTI,—the world's leading developer of research-based, validated assessment tools—done among engineering students describes two types of emerging entrepreneurs.[5] TTI calls the first type entrepreneurial-minded people. They like to be part of organized teams working together to achieve a goal, and they enjoy consistency. Having control is not of great importance to them.

Potential serial entrepreneurs form the second group. These are people who have a desire to own a business, perhaps because they want control. They thrive in having ultimate control over their life and business, and they tend to be more individualistic and have a greater sense of urgency.

They are happy to set direction and course for a company or team, but they need to feel that their own destiny is not limited, and thus, they must be managed carefully so as not to take the drive from them and risk losing them.

Entrepreneurs—whether EMPs (entrepreneurial-minded people) or serial—already possess the behaviors, attitudes, and values to build successful businesses independently or as employees within an organization. Finding the entrepreneurs (of either type) within the workforce and empowering them will allow leaders to work with their unique approach and reap the benefits for their company and society.

So how can they be identified? Unfortunately, degrees are not necessarily an indication. Instead, look for those traits that separate them from the general population and are typical of budding entrepreneurs.

Serial Entrepreneurs

There is a subset within entrepreneurs that is normally called serial entrepreneurs. This group is defined as those who have created more than one successful business that employs others. Like with most things in life, experience is a valuable asset in entrepreneurship. Those who have done it before have a better chance of success than first-time entrepreneurs do.

Previous experience helps entrepreneurs achieve faster growth and higher profitability, as well as sustained growth. The main reason for this higher success appears to be the use of a critical set of best practices developed from their first experience. When you start your first business, you think that it is your technical ability that matters, but the second time around you realize that it is the ability to run a business that really matters.

According to a study by TTI Performance Systems Ltd, these serial entrepreneurs potentially have three to five times the economic impact of a person who will be classified as an entrepreneur or small-business owner because:

- they have already experienced success and likely failure too;
- they learned from both, developing the professional skills vital for success;
- they may have personal funds from previous businesses, or they may have the ability to raise funds because of their past success and experience;
- their track record makes them more likely to create companies that tend to grow more and faster and employ more people; and
- in most cases, they have demonstrated the ability to sustain a business past the start-up phase and into the higher-growth job production years.[8]

Having said that, it is also common to find serial entrepreneurs who have failed in one or more ventures but persistently apply their experience to found businesses that become successful.

TTI examined the attitudes that motivate serial entrepreneurs using six value areas that we all hold with varying degrees of importance. A person's values tell us why they hold certain attitudes and why they choose to act as they do. These values are the motivators for our behavior.

The study identified the primary values of serial entrepreneurs as follows:

- those with a drive for a practical return on time or money spent to generate wealth or power (64 percent—mean for US adult population = 38 percent);
- those with a drive for knowledge, continuous learning, and discovery of new things (23 percent—mean for US adult population = 15 percent); and
- those with a drive for personal power, influence, and control over their environment (9 percent—mean for US adult population = 9 percent).

Considering that values drive behaviors, it shows that serial entrepreneurs are significantly more driven for a return on investment than the average US population. Translated, this means that serial entrepreneurs are always looking for the most efficient and effective way to conduct business. They are very practical in the decision-making process and remain focused on achieving a profitable bottom line.

Those with a drive for knowledge are motivated to be continuously learning about their business's industry and competition to find the best possible solution to issues. These entrepreneurs are motivated to keep up with the latest technological advances that affect their businesses.

Somewhat surprising is the result that says that serial

entrepreneurs are no different from the general population in the drive for personal power. These are people who gravitate toward positions of leadership in their quest for personal power.

The study also looked at the behavior of the subjects by examining what is easily observable in their day-to-day activities. It looked at their primary behavior and found that most serial entrepreneurs fall into the following categories:

- very competitive (57 percent—mean for US adult population = 12 percent)
- high trust (23 percent—mean for US adult population = 20 percent)
- quick to change (9 percent—mean for US adult population = 1 percent)
- rule breaker (6 percent—mean for US adult population = 12 percent)

The significant deviation of serial entrepreneurs is obviously in their highly competitive nature. The common setbacks that most start-ups suffer are sufficient to deter others, but serial entrepreneurs will stand up to the inconveniences and persevere to success. This competitiveness is the source of their resilience.

A serial entrepreneur can then be described as having the following characteristics:

- forward-looking
- values time
- enjoys challenges
- highly competitive
- self-starter
- innovative—challenges the status quo
- tenacious

- creative problem solver
- motivator for others
- negotiates conflicts
- independent—a rule breaker
- optimistic and enthusiastic

A serial entrepreneur then is somebody who is highly motivated to achieve and resilient enough to succeed, in part because they have the flexibility and decisiveness to adapt to the frequent change inherent in growth. The research also showed that serial entrepreneurs had these behaviors, attitudes, and values prior to building their first business.

They tend to be competitive, self-motivated, and very optimistic about their potential and the success of the business. They are, perhaps, not detail-oriented (unless they are engineers), but they motivate others to follow their vision and will go through obstacles to reach their goals.

They had the required traits before they built their first business, so they probably did not develop these traits while working on their various ventures, but surely they developed professional skills in the process.

From my experience: I always claim that in my many entrepreneurial ventures I learned the "what to do" but more importantly I learned the "what not to do" in business. Is this experience of setbacks and even failures that give serial entrepreneurs the winning hand when creating new businesses.

Self-Employed Entrepreneurs

There is another subgroup that is classified as entrepreneurs in some circles, but in fact, these people are in business by themselves and not necessarily aiming to create a sizable enterprise. These people are self-employed, and while they may have one or more employees, they run their businesses as an occupation—or sometimes more like a hobby—rather than as a bona fide business.

These people typically go into business because they are good at something. They can be carpenters, plumbers, mechanics, attorneys (yes, attorneys), accountants, hairdressers, or anything else, and they want to be their own boss, so they go into business by themselves. The truth is that these people do not really run a business; they simply go to work at a job that they installed and work for a boss that they chose.

They do not know what they do not know, and this can be scary when you realize that there is an unknown world out there. You do not know what it is and what challenges it presents. Worse yet is when you feel that you have a nice position and that you would have to risk it to go into the unknown.

Likely, at one time, they had the entrepreneurial dream; they were technicians suffering from what Michael Gerber calls an "entrepreneurial seizure."[6] Once they started their business, however, they changed the lofty dream for a terror of heights. They are happy working for themselves and not worrying about creating a sizable company. They realize that they do not fit the real entrepreneurial mold.

From my experience: One time I was recruiting a lawyer as a potential member for a peer-advisory board I was chairing. He told me: "I don't have a business; I have a law practice." To which I replied, "Oh, I see. Tell me, do you have employees?" And he said he did. I asked, "Do you have HR issues?" And he said, "Boy, do I!" I continued: "Do you do marketing?" He admitted he did to recruit clients. I asked, "Do you deal with banks, profit-and-loss statements, balance sheets, accounts payable, accounts receivable…"

He interrupted me, saying, "OK, OK. I see where you're going. I have a business don't I?" I said, "Your business is not different than any others; it is just called a different name, but you have the same issues that any other business owner has." He joined the advisory board, and after a few months, he told me: "You were right; my business has the same issues as any of the others." So, yes, lawyers also have their own business.

The Young Potential Entrepreneurs

Millennials (generation Y) are said to be lazy, impatient, demanding, and a few other adjectives that are not very glamorous. However, those same qualities can make them prime suspects to enter the entrepreneurial ranks.

Being impatient, they want everything, and they want it now. A sign of this is apparent in the decline of the sport of golf that many attribute to the lack of interest by youngsters. The number of people playing golf has declined by 24 percent in the last few years, and it is said that young people shy from it because they see the sport a being elitist and too time-intensive.

They do not want to go through a learning or adaptation period, and while this can be a negative for entrepreneurship, depending on circumstances, it can also be a positive. They tend not to play by the rules and do what they need to do to get ahead.

They have self-confidence almost to an excess, and this is a great trait to make it as an entrepreneur as long as it is contained. Entrepreneurs need to believe in their vision and in their dreams, and gen Y craving the limelight can definitely help them gain self-confidence to reach their vision and goals.

Rather than taking their concentration away from business-related activities, their obsession with all social media gives them excellent opportunities for networking. Being so digitally savvy gives them an advantage when using the latest technology for improving their business. They also have access to programs and services not available to previous generations in the entrepreneurial stage.

Being young and aggressive, generation Y has the energy to build a business, despite inevitable obstacles. In addition, since they are young, they likely do not have extra responsibilities, like family and mortgages and, thus, can concentrate more on the business.

If we accept that gen Y has high potential as entrepreneurs, what about generation Z (those born between 1994 and 2010, which means that they are now, at best, in high school)? The "Internet generation," as it is known, is even more digitally savvy than gen Y and should be able to take advantage of this trait as entrepreneurs.

In a study called "High School Careers," Shore Consulting surveyed students in high school and college and found that 72 percent of high-school students and 64 percent of college students claim they want to start a business as soon as possible.[7]

Additionally, they reported that 61 percent of high-school students and 43 percent of college students would rather be entrepreneurs than employees in some corporation when they graduate from college. We do not know what their financial burden will be after college, but we do know that gen Y is loaded with a trillion dollars in student loans. If this parameter is taken out of the equation for gen Z people, they will be freer to follow their dreams and start businesses.

From my experience: *I have three sons and they are examples of the various types of entrepreneurship discussed.*

Son number one inherited my entrepreneurship; he created a successful business when he was 19 years old, and after the expected ups-and-downs typical of entrepreneurship, he created another successful business. Son number two became an intrapreneur who provided value to his employers and later became a coach and adviser to small business owners within the sphere of a large organization. Son number three chose the self-employed route in occupations that he enjoys. This illustrates that even within a family, different personalities adapt to different approaches to business entrepreneurship.

Too Old or Too Young?

When is someone too young or too old to start a company? There are no age limits or even recommended ages to increase the chances of success, except to have enough experience and knowledge to ensure the viability of the venture. There are plenty of examples at both end of the spectrum of people who became entrepreneurs, started, and run companies very successfully.

There are, of course, the famous cases such as Harlan Sanders starting KFC at age 65, and the numerous high-tech companies started by young men and women during their college years or soon thereafter, but they are not unique. Many others, albeit not as well known, have also joined the ranks of successful entrepreneurs either at an early age or at a moderately advanced age.

Funders and Founders show in its website—www.fundersandfounders.com—representative charts illustrating it. To the already mentioned group of early-twenties high-techies, there seems to follow a peak of people in the mid-thirties and then one of early forties business adventurers. However, the data indicates that entrepreneurship is not set by age, but by the drive to reach a goal.

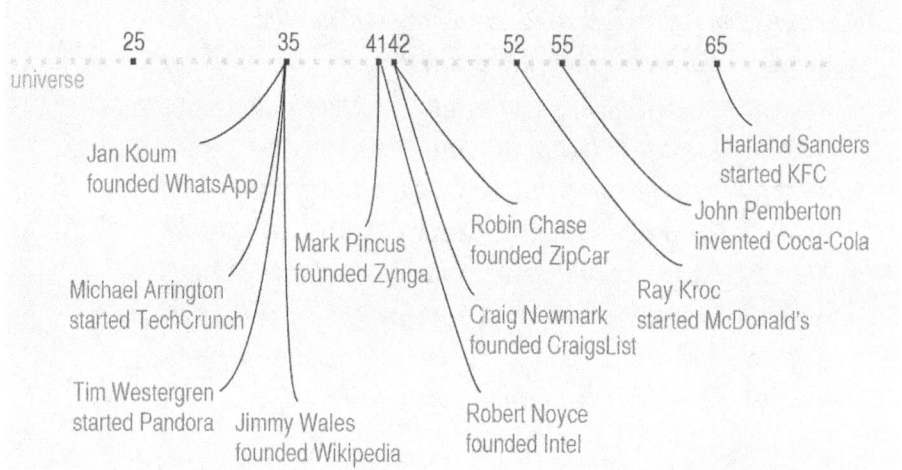

Partial graph taken from the Funders and Founders website.

There are pluses and minuses to both extremes. Young entrepreneurs may have a perceived advantage of enthusiasm and energy, while older entrepreneurs have more experience and likely more acquired knowledge. Nevertheless, the traits of each person are what determine the ultimate success, not how young or old the person is.

From my experience: In my own case, I started businesses at very young age and I also started some later in life. My latest venture was starting a business at 59 and it became perhaps my most enjoyable one. As a CEO coach I worked with several business owners who became entrepreneurs at an age when other people are thinking of enjoying retirement. Usually, these business impresarios are among the most successful ones.

Part II

Are You a Player?

"Your time is limited, so don't waste it living someone else's life. Don't be trapped by dogma – which is living with the results of other people's thinking. Don't let the noise of other's opinions drown out your own inner voice. And most important, have the courage to follow your heart and intuition. They somehow already know what you truly want to become. Everything else is secondary."
- Steve Jobs

Chapter III – Can You Play?

Do You Have What It Takes?

Although it wasn't always like this, entrepreneurship is glorified in our society. Thirty, forty, or fifty years ago, starting a business was looked at as a very risky journey, and leaving the comfort of employment was only for high adventurers. It became not only accepted but even desired when the high rollers of the 1970s and '80s were seen as big winners. As the small-business community grew, going into business by oneself became a popular thing to do.

> *My own experience: I left IBM (mother IBM I called it) where I was having a very successful career to become one of the founders of a high-profile startup. This was almost unheard of; leaving such a comfortable position to go into a highly risky situation was looked at as a sin. To make it even more risky, the startup company was in competition with IBM in a highly technical field. It was probably a crazy thing to do, but the lessons I learned from that adventure amply justified the move. My entrepreneurial personality—already formed from long before—continued to grow as a result of that experience.*

The fact is that people should be what they want to be and can be. Not everyone can be a doctor, an astronaut, a teacher, or a plumber, and certainly not everyone has what it takes to be a business owner or desire the risk of entrepreneurship. And if you don't have *it*, don't even try the business ownership world, because you will be frustrated and may even go broke.

So if you decide to become an entrepreneur, you will be in a select group of individuals who contribute to the well-being of the country (and the world). And if your business survives and is successful, you will be in an even more select group.

But how or why do you decide you want to be an entrepreneur? It can be for one of many reasons that are personal or business/employment driven. It can stem from the birth of a child, graduating from college, a change of location, meeting the right partner, and a million others circumstances.

On the business/employment side, it could be because of a bad or good experience as an employee, you do not like your boss, you do not feel you are given the value you deserve, you lost your job, you feel you know more than your employer, or many other reasons. Whatever the reason, it lighted a flame that will not be easily extinguished.

In my particular case—as it may be with many of you—I believe I was born with the entrepreneurial mark. My first experience as an entrepreneur was when I was only thirteen years old, and by the time I started my professional career, I had had several entrepreneurial experiences. But the decisive reasons that took me away from the employment ranks were a combination of not being happy as an employee and the realization that I had to do it to be happy. I gave up a great career and a lot of money (for some time), but I gained enormous self-satisfaction.

Inc.500's survey of its top companies asked the owners why they decided to start their businesses.[8] The answers were:

- entrepreneurship suited my skills and abilities: 29 percent
- I wanted to be my own boss: 20 percent
- I had an idea, and I just had to try it: 18 percent
- I wanted financial success: 11 percent

- I admired other entrepreneurs and wanted to emulate them: 9 percent
- other reasons: 13 percent

In my coaching career and running peer-advisory boards for many years, I worked with a great variety of business owners, and the self-stated reasons that made them entrepreneurs are as different as their businesses, but there is commonality in their traits and drive. The personalities are very different too, but all of them wouldn't change the hardships of business ownership for anything. When asked if having to do it over again would they, unanimously they would respond with an emphatic yes.

Whether their enterprise is a family business, a solo experience, a partnership, a subset of a large operation, participating in a technical field, a manufacturing or distribution or sales or professional or any other field, they recognize the shortcomings and sacrifices of being business owners, but they relish the experience and congratulate themselves for choosing that route.

What Are You Risking?

You need to know that the life of an entrepreneur can be isolated and demanding to the point that the family life suffers. A business owner owes his life to the business. As a business owner, you have the privilege of working an enormous amount of hours, skipping weekends, and giving up sleep. The Inc.500 survey claimed that the owners of those companies worked more than a hundred hours a week in the first year of the venture. The obvious consequence is that the private life suffers, and with it the family environment.

It is also a lonely life. The entrepreneur is the all-around everything during the start-up phase of the business, and even after an organization begins to take shape, the loneliness continues. People who are comfortably employed and enjoy the camaraderie of sharing time with other employees or being part of a team or an organization would miss that environment and will find it difficult to adjust to the loneliness of entrepreneurship.

In corporate life, typically one has the support of other parts of the organization (HR, maintenance, engineering, production, etc.), and it can be depressing to face the reality of having nobody to get help from or even talk to.

Sadly, as the title of one of my book states, it's lonely at the top, regardless of the size of the organization.[9] That is because, as the top dog, you must make or at least participate in all decisions, and there are some issues that you cannot discuss with others. The buck stops at your desk, and there is a tremendous feeling of isolation as a result.

In some businesses, husband and wife work together as partners. Clearly this helps with the feeling of loneliness because the two support each other and share those issues that cannot be discussed with others, however, unless strict rules are set and applied, this arrangement can be deteriorating to married life.

I have worked with entrepreneurial couples who spend many hours working in the business together. When husband and wife spend that much time together in the business, chances are that they carry the business talk to their house, drastically reducing any other type of communication. The most likely result is damage to the husband-wife relationship.

From my experience: *I worked with a couple who owned a successful business but that was going through a* *significant down cycle. As a result both husband and wife worked extremely long hours together and even when they were at home the conversation always centered on the business. Life as a couple practically disappeared and, not surprisingly, they started to grow apart in the marriage while sharing everything as business partners. The thought of a separation or divorce crossed their minds but did not progress because of the uncertainty of what to do with the company if they separated.*

My job as their coach was to make them realize that the business was still viable and had enormous potential, and that their work habits were not being helpful to the business (and obviously to the marriage). I convinced them to focus on the long term and not just in the present. More importantly, I assigned specific jobs for each of them, got them to leave the business at reasonable hours and prodded them to go out as a couple at least one night a week and to take at least two weekends off every month.

Although reluctantly, they accepted my advice and changed their work and personal routines and the results became palpable within a short time. Today the business is thriving with several times higher top and bottom lines, and they are a happy couple again.

It is imperative to the couple's marriage to agree on certain restraining practices regarding hours of work, partnership responsibilities, methods of communicating, and, most importantly, relationship outside the business. It is also critical for them to agree on the actual emotional value of the business in relation to the family and to be realistic as to the present and future of the business.

From my experience: *Although somewhat different from the description above, it illustrates the point. My* *wife was the entrepreneur in this case. She owned a small chain of retail stores and our oldest son was a manager at one of the stores. The conversations at home always revolved around what was happening in the business, particularly at dinner time despite the presence of three other children. One day my son—in a very powerful way—said: what are we doing? This is not a family; this is a business council. My wife and I looked at each other and realized that we were creating a barrier within the family. At that point we decided that business talk was prohibited at dinner time, and we "became a family" once again.*

So, considering all of the above…

Are You (Can You Be) an Entrepreneur?

Do you have the potential to be successful?

I believe that everyone has the potential deep inside them, but to be successful, that potential has to come to the surface.

To be an entrepreneur, business acumen or technical capability is not enough—one must have the right personality and social and psychological makeup. It takes a special type of person to have the vision, drive, dedication, endurance, enthusiasm, toughness, and self-motivation that entrepreneurship requires. What makes an entrepreneur is not knowing everything about business but being passionate about the vision and fearless enough to make it happen.

Of all the traits required to be an entrepreneur, vision stands out as, perhaps, the most important. Vision is what drives an entrepreneur and a business owner; without it, the motivation to start and nurture a business is an aimless effort to get to an undefined destination. The vision of what it can be or how far it can go is the big motivator that keeps the entrepreneurial fire going.

Ben Horowitz claims that, as a venture capitalist, what he looks for in an entrepreneur is a combination of great genius and courage. He adds that "the genius part is self-evident as a requirement to be a successful entrepreneur, but the courage part is less obvious. However, no other quality—no vision, no creativity, no charisma—is more essential to succeed as an entrepreneur."[10]

The life of an entrepreneur is filled with questions: How much does it cost? What can we charge? What is the margin? By when? What dictates most of the actions is the quickest route to revenues and profits. Adversities are to be expected as part of the entrepreneurial game; be prepared to face them and beat them.

If you are used to working in the comfort of large organizations, you may find it very difficult to adapt to the loneliness or near loneliness of a start-up. In a large company, one can count on varied and comprehensive support in many areas of a business, but as an entrepreneur in a start-up, you are required to fly solo many times. Being the all-around worker and master of everything is a typical job definition in a start-up and even in an embryonic company.

I am fortunate in that I can adapt very easily in a small company or in a large company. I have started businesses and worked in several start-ups. I went from start-ups to a huge company like IBM, to a start-up followed by another large company, and then to my own business again (multiple times) and working with dozens of small-business owners.

But this flexibility is not for everyone; in fact, most people are either subjects of secure employment (preferably in sizable companies) or risk takers willing to chance it as entrepreneurs. My adaptability has given me the opportunity to learn both ends of the spectrum.

My advice to owners of small businesses is to beware of hiring employees who have worked only in large companies, because the big-company syndrome is hard to shake loose, and those who can adapt and perform well in a small company are rare, indeed.

Is Entrepreneurship for You?

Entrepreneurs are found in all fields of industry and commerce, and even in education and government. While it is common to see entrepreneurial ventures in certain industries—such as high-tech—the entrepreneurial spirit knows no bounds, and it is only limited by the imagination of the entrepreneurs.

In his recently published book, *Hunting in a Farmer's World: Celebrating the Mind of an Entrepreneur*, my friend and colleague John Dini classifies entrepreneurs as hunters while the rest of the population are farmers.[11]

He explains the differences this way: in business, entrepreneurs hunt for ideas, solutions, new ways of doing things, new markets, and new customers; farmers, on the other hand, are those who do the yearly planning, budgeting, and standardizing and make sure things are organized and people are doing what they are supposed to be doing.

Hunters build companies with vision, creativity, and tenacity; they do not concern themselves (at least at the beginning in start-up mode) with policies and procedures (although they probably should). They need to be free from routine activities so that they can concentrate on creating, improving, designing, and forming.

Starting your own business can be an exciting and rewarding experience. It can offer numerous advantages, such as being your own boss, setting your own schedule, and making a living doing something you enjoy. But it is not always glamorous (it seldom is) and requires sacrifices, hard work, and a heavy dose of creativity and planning.

As an entrepreneur, you must be comfortable with high risk and uncertainty, thus, if you can't tolerate high risk, entrepreneurship is not for you. You will be risking not only money but also intangibles, such as reputation, time, and the opportunity to do other things at your reach (a better job, a move to another city that you would like to live in, etc.).

If you want to start a business, it must be because you believe in something that you have, whether it is a thing (a product), an idea, or just a desire to do it. And if you BELIEVE in it (just like that, in capital letters), you must have the passion to make it a reality. Passion is not only a requirement but an important asset that you can count on to be successful in a venture.

Ralph Waldo Emerson said, "Passion is the most powerful engine of success. When you do a thing, do it with all your might. Put your whole soul into it. Stamp it with your own personality. Be active; be energetic and faithful, and you will accomplish your object. Nothing great was ever achieved without passion."[12]

Emerson said, "Stamp it with your own personality," and this is critical because we are all different, and what works for someone may not work for others. Your personality dictates how you must apply your passion to be successful. You need to recognize your passion and nurture it as you implement your dream.

Are You Ready for the Big Game?

We must distinguish between being an entrepreneur and being self-employed. As a self-employed person, you have a job, but you are not really an entrepreneur. But if you have the dream and what it takes to be an entrepreneur, you can be affected by the entrepreneurial seizure as Michael Gerber calls it. It can hit someone without warning, and it can happen for a variety of reasons…and there is no cure for it.

Once you are affected by it, you will never be the same. The thought of independence will always be with you, either in the forefront or in the background, but it will be there, telling you that, perhaps, there is a better way to live.

Be careful, be aware of the desire, and think carefully before making it the great motivator or reason to live. Analyze your personality, traits, qualifications, potential, assets, risk tolerance, ability to support—and endure—a period of building the business (likely with no or little income), and family situation.

Do much research regarding the market for your products or services, the competition, the financial environment, and the availability of the resources that you will need (materials, people, equipment, physical space, etc.). Most of all, do a deep evaluation of yourself to learn if you are a good candidate for the position.

Do you have what it takes? Are you interested in being a business owner/entrepreneur, or are you happy being employed? As a coach, I have seen many people wanting to get into business without the capabilities or personality to do it. Some think that, by having the necessary funds and becoming familiar with the legal, tax, and administration issues, they are ready to emerge as business owners and conquer the world.

Some believe that becoming self-employed classifies them as entrepreneurs or businesspeople, but the reality is very different because entrepreneurship requires much more than the desire to have your own business. Not understanding this can transform the entrepreneurial dream into a business nightmare.

Some believe that, by knowing the technical (or trade) side of a business, they understand a company that does technical work, and that cannot be further from the truth. This happens to be the root cause of many business failures, and it is typical of technicians who start a business. Running a business requires proficiency—or at least a basic knowledge—of many areas, such as accounting, sales, operations management, and so on.

Being an entrepreneur and building a business is much like boxing in that it is hard, lonely, and demands constant and vigilant focus. Regardless of how well you do, you must be ready to get punched again by the demands of the business and its problems. And if you get knocked down, you must get up and face the danger and the excitement again.

As Horowitz said, "In business, as in boxing, you get hit, and it is painful, but then you take a breather, and you are ready for the next round." Are you ready to be a fighter?

Ask yourself the following questions, and your answers will guide you to the truth about entrepreneurship.

- Am I willing to invest the money, time, and effort to start and run a business?
- Am I able to function in an environment of uncertainty?
- Do I have the ability to overcome difficult obstacles?
- Do I understand my own limitations, as well as my strengths?
- Am I able to cure my weaknesses while emphasizing my strengths?
- Am I easily discouraged?
- Am I willing to sacrifice many things to reach my dream of entrepreneurship?

- Am I willing to dedicate an enormous amount of time on a consistent basis?
- Am I willing to risk my financial assets?
- Is my family willing to put up with me during the difficult times of business creation?
- Is my work history commensurate with being an entrepreneur?
- Am I willing and able to let go by delegating when it becomes necessary?
- What am I good at? (Consider that there is much more to owning a business than just knowing how to do something.)
- Am I detail-oriented or a big-picture person?
- Am I a self-starter, or do I need prodding?
- Do I have/want work-life balance? Can I happily work twelve hours per day seven days per week?
- What is my definition of success? How much money do I need/want?
- How good am I at making key decisions? Do I need support to make them? Do I need consensus?

But perhaps the most important question to ask yourself is:

- Why do I want to do this? What is the inspiration driving me?
  - Is it a lifelong dream or desperation to do something different?
  - Is it because I want to make a lot of money?
  - Is it because I want to have a good life?
  - Is it because I want to have lots of time for other things?
  - Is it because I want to be famous?
  - Is it because I have a fantastic product that people will want?

o   Is it to prove to others or to myself that I can do it?

And another key question to ask yourself is: am I a visionary?

A visionary is a strategic thinker with workable ideas who sees the big picture and is in tune with the market and the industry and the financial environment in which to operate. A visionary/entrepreneur is typically good with relationships, solving problems, creating the vision for the business, and having the strength to pursue that vision. Visionaries are creators.

The other side of the visionary coin is that they are not good at details, don't like the boring side of the business (administrative, management, legal, etc.), and they are not good at delegating or holding people accountable. If you decide to start a business, you must be the visionary and continue to be it as the business grows, but you will also need to learn to be a manager and a leader.

Before deciding to embark in business ownership, new entrepreneurs must have at least a working knowledge of the basics of business management. The following list is by no means exhaustive, but it represents a good sample of items that all business owners must feel comfortable knowing.

- accounting/finance: how to read and interpret profit and losses and balance-sheet statements; know the significance of financial ratios, difference between cash flow and accounting, difference between operating funds and capital funds, how to prepare a budget, relationship between accounts-payable days and accounts-receivable days, and how to finance accounts receivable

- taxes: requirements for tax compliance, including income tax, sales tax, payroll taxes, and how to report them
- planning: business, marketing, sales, operations, and strategic plans and developing sales and profit projections and adjusting all plans to fit projections
- human resources: hiring plan, how to select and hire employees, organization development, personnel management, and legal issues involved
- marketing/advertising: understanding what they are and having a plan and a budget to maximize the benefits of targeted marketing and advertising
- operations: manufacturing cost, direct versus indirect costs, overhead costs, labor rate, work flow, inventory control, quality control, reliability control, resource management, supply chains, equipment selection and maintenance, material handling, etc.

It will also help to know:
- the difference between customer service (making the costumer happy) and quality process (doing it right the first time);
- and promote what makes you and your product or service unique or special compared to the competition;
- to think like an owner instead of an employee (the ability to operate what you created with your entrepreneurial vision);
- international and global opportunities and threats that may exist for your product or service;
- how to take advantage of the Internet and electronic communications; and
- challenges and opportunities of e-commerce and how to maximize advantages of technology available.

You can be sure that, at some point, you will be faced with these issues, and they will rob time from your busy schedule. You need to realize that this is part of the knowledge required, and consequently, you need to plan for it.

Think carefully about all the questions and issues listed—and many others that I am not listing but would be important to you—and analyze your answers, trying to be as neutral as possible regarding your dream.

As a business owner, many times you will feel alone and with nobody to go to for help; it's lonely at the top. You will feel that nobody will understand your problems and help you find answers. You cannot go to your employees because they will see a sign of weakness. You cannot go to your family or your financial institutions because they will be frightened. You will want to show strength even though you are scared. You know you must move forward, but you are not sure how.

It is important then, if you decide that you want to start a business, to have a support system in place. As a business owner, you will have to make many important decisions, not just in the start-up phase but on an ongoing basis—at least until you are able to have an organization in place. It can also be very helpful to have a business mentor who is experienced, successful, and willing to provide advice and guidance.

I also highly recommend joining a peer-advisory board where you will meet with a group of other business owners to exchange ideas and get support from the group. Each member benefits from the collective experience of all members and of the facilitator/coach. Typically on these boards, the members meet privately with the coach, who helps them with business-related issues. (See the appendix).

Some reasons entrepreneurs fail:

- lack of capital (money)
- lack of planning
- lack the personality traits
- lack of business planning
- poor business sense
- lack of strategic planning
- not able to cope with problems
- lack of realistic planning
- can't accept risks
- lack of sensible planning

Some reasons entrepreneurs succeed:

- have the right personal characteristics and attributes
- go into business for the right reasons
- listen to advice from knowledgeable people
- start with a good business plan
- have sufficient capital
- surround themselves with the right people
- are resilient and never give up
- are good leaders
- are not afraid to admit when they are wrong
- plan, plan, plan, and then plan some more
- execute, execute, execute the plan

My repeated insistence in planning is not exaggerated or capricious; I list various planning tasks as necessary in any business. It was said that "running a business without the proper planning is like driving a vehicle looking only at the rear-view mirror; you know where you have been, but you do not know where you are going."

Chapter IV – Get Fit For the Game

Questions Before Starting a Business

If you want to start a business, make sure you analyze the reality of your dream and its practicality.

- Is your idea good enough? (Just because it sounds good to you does not mean that the market will agree.)
  - Is there a need for your product or service?
  - Is the market large enough?
  - What is the competition?
  - Is there uniqueness in your product or service?

- How well can you execute the concept? (A great idea does not translate into a business without great execution.)
  - Is the product or service ready to be marketed?
  - Can you produce it easily and profitably?
  - Do you have the resources necessary?
  - How will you market it?

- Is your business model practical and profitable? (To have a chance at success, your business approach must ensure profitability.)
  - What will it cost to produce the product or provide the service?
  - What is the cost of sales and marketing?
  - Whom are you selling to?
  - How will you sell, i.e., direct, to individuals, to businesses, online?

These are only an example of the questions you need to

answer before making the decision to embark on the adventure of business ownership. The answers to these questions (and many others) must form part of the business plan that will guide the formation of the business.

Next, if you have made up your mind to move forward, ask yourself the following questions to make sure you have considered these key business decisions:

- What kind of business do I want?
- What legal structure of my business is recommended?
- Who is my ideal customer?
- Am I prepared to spend the time and money needed to get my business off the ground?
- How will I compete, and what makes my business and products or services different?
- How many employees will I need, and when?
- What types of suppliers do I need?
- Can these suppliers provide the products and support that I need?
- How much money do I need to get started and during the start-up phase?
- Would a bank be sympathetic to my needs if I need to get a loan?
- How soon can I have my products or services ready to be offered?
- How long do I have until I start making a profit, and will I have enough money until then?
- How will I price my product or service, and will it be competitive?
- What kind of insurance do I need?
- How will I manage my business?
- How vulnerable are my family's assets?

- What will happen if I become unable to manage the business because of a disability or, worse yet, death?
- What would be my exit strategy? (It is never too soon to think about this because of the point above.)
- What is my plan B if things do not go right?

Perhaps the money issues should be at the top of the list—not just money for the business but, even more importantly, funds for personal and family expenses. Not having a solid backup in the personal accounts presents a high risk in two forms: jeopardizing family well-being (and even integrity) and affecting concentration in business matters. The latter occurs if the entrepreneur is concerned over family money issues and he or she cannot be fully concentrated on the business.

Thus, before starting a new venture, it is imperative to have a safe cushion of cash for personal and family expenses. The size of this cushion can vary depending on a number of factors, i.e., the type of venture, the expected time before the venture is profitable (and the entrepreneur can start drawing a salary), personal and family needs, and the risks involved.

Of course, money management requires large doses of discipline, both in the business and of the family funds. By this, I mean that one cannot be tempted to borrow from the personal accounts to cover business emergencies, and vice versa. One of the first steps should be to develop a realistic budget for the business (and, perhaps, also for the family) and to religiously stick to it as best as possible. Revisions to the budget should be judicious and infrequent.

Many new business owners keep one checking account, and they use it for business and personal expenses. Besides the legal and tax ramifications that this can have, it is impossible to be able to manage the business this way. With this practice, the owner does not know the real cost of doing business and, consequently, the true bottom line.

One of the most critical questions you must ask yourself has to do with the financing of the business. Are you a "bootstrapper" or do you plan to seek investors? If your goal is to have maximum control of the business and of the equity, yo want to finance growth from internally generated profits; in other words, you are prepared to bootstrap your venture.

However, if you are more interested in faster growth while limiting your personal risk, you may want to consider recruiting investors. Seven percent of the Inc 500 companies are venture backed, compared to just two percent of general small businesses, meaning that 98 percent of all small businesses are bootstrapped.

Bootstrapping means having a sharp focus on cash flow, reducing expenses and maximizing accounts receivable, which creates a more fundamentally sound company. Bootstrapping is hard and requires much discipline, but as a reward the owner gets to keep full ownership and all of the equity.

The same Inc.500 survey quoted earlier also asked the owners of the top companies what were the sources of their start-up capital. The answers varied.

- savings: 71 percent
- loans from friends and family: 21 percent
- personal bank loans: 13 percent
- home-equity loans or lines of credit: 12 percent
- angel funding: 9 percent
- venture capital (VC): 6 percent
- SBA guaranteed loans: 3 percent

This illustrates the fact that most small-business

entrepreneurs finance their start-ups with money of their own or from family and friends. They are risking not only their financial well-being but also their family security.

Another important subject covered by the same survey was what their biggest challenge was in the first year.

- shortage of capital: 45 percent
- bad fit with other key employees: 16 percent
- didn't test product enough: 13 percent
- spent too much money: 11 percent
- bad fit with partner: 10 percent
- spent too much time trying to raise money: 3 percent
- bad fit with investor: 2 percent

A key consideration before launching the business needs to be the readiness of the market for the product the company will sell. Is the market ready? Is the product ready? Was all the testing of the product and of the market completed? Do not start investing in building your company until you can answer these questions positively.

Conversely, do not spend so much time perfecting your product so that, when you are finally ready, the market window has closed. I always say that you can perfect a product to the point of obsolescence. There has to be a judgment call on the difference between market ready and the need to perfect.

> ***From my experience:*** *I consulted for a startup that had a great promising product; an advanced technology in the consumer's marketplace with extraordinary applications. The founders invested a substantial amount of money, hired several engineers, vice presidents of sales, engineering and production, and traveled to the Far East to woo potential investors. All this with the expectations that*

investors would flock in attracted by the product.

Unfortunately the technology was not as ready as promoted and it became obvious when demonstrating the prototypes. In addition, the supposedly ready market was not as ready as they thought and there were doubts as to its eventual readiness. After unsuccessfully courting VCs and Angels(individual investors), money ran out and the entrepreneurs were forced to close the business resulting in major losses of money, loss of jobs for everyone hired in the enthusiastic mode, and even some lawsuits for breach of contracts.

If the developers of the technology would have been honest about its status and the hired engineers would have evaluated it consciously, and if the principals would have done a true analysis of the market rather than looking at it with embellished eyes, they could have prevented all this pain and bad experience

Starting a Business

The market will always welcome better, faster and smarter way to do things and the products to achieve it. Fortunately, there is lots of room for improvement in existing products, meaning that there are many opportunities to explore by new entrepreneurs.

If you are committed to starting a business focus on things that the market wants, not just in a nice product. You must focus on doing something different and better; something that consumers expect and demand and that will make a difference in the market.

Because of the many variables involved, it is impossible to

have a list of fundamental steps to cover when starting a business. However, a few "must do" steps are mandatory.

Know yourself. Following the advice in this book do a good self-examination of your strengths and weaknesses, your goals, your reasons for wanting to go into business, and your expectations. This step is not supposed to dissuade you from the adventure; rather it is to get you to start thinking and planning.

Know your purpose. Why are you going into business? What needs does your startup address? Why will people be interested in your business? Why will people be interested in your product or service?

Know your industry. Evaluate your idea of a product or service. Who will buy it? Who will be your competitors? How is your product or service better than the competition? How are you better than your competitors? What is the market size? What portion of the market can you capture?

Know your business model. How will you sell? How will you fabricate the product or provide the service? How much will it cost to produce them? How long before you can make a profit or break even? What resources do you need and what do you have?

Know your operating plan. This is your roadmap to success and as such, it must be well throughout and, more importantly, executed. Your plan will tell you what you need to do in order to achieve your goals and will help you chart your progress. Your plan must be a dynamic document that you update as business conditions change, not a static piece that you put on a shelf and never use again.

Know your resources. What do you need and what do you

have? Will you get outside funding or bootstrap it? Analyze your needs and decide what is best for your situation. Do you have the facilities that you need? Do you have the materials and equipment that you need?

And also follow these acumens:

If you do it, do it because you enjoy it. If your heart is not in it, the temptations to abandon it will be high in difficult times. Doing something you love you are motivated to endure difficulties.

Believe in your venture. It is important that you believe in what do you and in yourself. Believing in you and in the venture, pumps self-motivation.

Learn from others. Take any opportunity to learn and improve your business and yourself as a welcome happening. You do not know what you do not know, so beware of becoming to complacent.

Serve your customer's needs, not yourself. The business is to serve the needs of your customers; keeping this in mind when making decisions, you will build a product that will make customers excited and will want to use it.

Anticipate what is coming. Although you cannot know for sure what new developments will be coming to the business world, you need to be aware of trends that may have an impact on your business.

Be flexible. You may have to face surprises when you least expect them and will need to react quickly. Flexibility will be an important trait for your business to have.

Be ready for hard work. As we already covered it in this book, hard work is what you must expect as a perquisite of owning your business. Have a life but be always ready to work hard.

Do not ever give up. Regardless of the challenges that you face, keep your spirits high and never, never give up.

Chapter V – Your Performance

The Life of a Business Owner

Owning a business has many advantages, and owners have many privileges, but there is also another side to the ownership coin. On the positive side, there is the pride and personal satisfaction of being the boss and not having to answer to anybody (except to customers, employees, investors, and other stakeholders…not to mention the IRS).

Financially it can have significant rewards, assuming the business is successful. Besides reaping the profits, the owner can shelter personal assets and even deduct from taxes some personal expenses that are also business expenses (ensuring they qualify as such). Choosing the right legal formation of the business can also have substantial tax advantages.

However, as a business owner, you also have the so-called privilege of working half days in which you can choose the half (which twelve-hour period within the twenty-four hours of each day). You are able to *donate* your weekends to the business. You can also have the privilege of deferring your salary so that you can pay your employees or the government.

As a big ego reward, you can give the company your name and give opposing attorneys in a lawsuit the reason to include you personally in collecting the awards from the suit.

You will also have the distinct honor of personally guaranteeing any bank loans that the company may need, so if you (or the business) default on the loan, you will not only lose the business assets but also your personal assets.

Your business, regardless of its type, will go through growth stages. If you are lucky and your vision drives it, the business will reach maturity, and with it, you will reach success. However, some businesses will get stuck in some of the early stages; mom-and-pop-type businesses will rarely go past a survival stage, and some—many unfortunately—will die there or in some other close stage.

As you start a business, likely you will start from zero, i.e., zero sales, zero revenues, zero profits, zero customers. But you have already invested a lot of money, time, and effort. You purchased equipment and furniture, rented space, and paid for all the incidentals needed to start.

You start getting stressed out because money flows out, but none is coming in, and your reserves are getting smaller by the day. Nevertheless, you are excited, and you move at a hundred miles per hour. You get a high when you sign your first customer; you get another high when you deliver your first product (or service). The highs follow, with receiving the first payment, hiring the first employee, etc.

A new revelation hits you, and that is that the business may be more than an extension of you—the owner—but you still can't accept the idea of not being completely in charge. Delegation is not in your vocabulary, and decision making is all yours.

You start to realize that you did not know it all, but you are learning and applying what you learn. You make adjustments, and things start improving. You get good feedback from customers; you are happy, and you are working more than ever, but you do it with a smile.

You need to rely on your creativity because business

conditions change so rapidly that what you thought was a well-planned business model can quickly become irrelevant without some key changes. Your ability to adjust on the go may save you.

Out of necessity, you realize that one of the keys to success is not having enough resources but being resourceful with what you have. If you do not have what you need, you need to somehow figure out how to get along without it.

Some problems arise; you get worried and redouble your efforts, and family life suffers because you spent too many hours at work or thinking about the business. But it is all part of the game, and you recognize it as such. Those pesky problems are fixed, and you get reenergized.

The business starts to grow nicely. As the business grows, your team grows too, and with it your HR problems—those that you hate so much but you need to deal with. You pay some debts, and that's a nice feeling. You start taking a small salary, and that's an even better feeling. You are on your way to success.

How long did this period take? It depends on a million things, and every business is different. Was it easy? Perhaps, and perhaps not, but surely it was stressful, exciting, painful, rewarding, discouraging, motivating, and a few other qualifiers, but looking back from your new perch of success, you would not change it for anything.

Next, you go to phase two. The company grows nicely, but your job doesn't get any easier. It is challenging but with a different twist—one with success in sight but with different issues that pop up daily: people, production, and financing issues. But at least you see payback to your twelve-hours-per-day routine.

In the start-up phase, you, the owner, are everything, but as the company grows, you start adding employees and financial resources. Now is the time to start structuring the operations so that success is not overly dependent on you alone. You need to realize now that the company won't fall apart if you are not there doing everything.

The next phase is totally different once again. Your job has changed. You are no longer the chief cook and bottle washer. You have become or are becoming a CEO. This is new for you, and you need to learn the job; you need to delegate and empower people, even if it is a difficult task for you. And—gosh this is difficult!—you need to hold people accountable.

The path to grow from business infancy (start-up) to adolescence presents some challenges that many owners find difficult to overcome while at the same time relishing the opportunity. It is in this phase that the owner must change to being the CEO (must be a leader from the beginning), and this is where a mentor or a coach can be most useful.

> *From my experience: I first started coaching a talented business owner when he was going through this phase. He confided in me that he did not feel capable to take the company to the next level. I disagreed with him and told him that he had the talent and capability to do it and only needed some coaching.*
>
> *Fast forward several years; his company has grown exponentially in all aspects and he is recognized as an excellent entrepreneur and leader. Coaching and his own realization of who he was and his strengths, made the difference and made him a winner.*

As the CEO and leader, you must create a culture that grows and develops its people. Validate your employees by involving them in management decisions. Allow employees to help develop the objectives and the strategic plan to achieve them. People will support what they helped create, so by involving them, you are helping the company grow.

Tough job, but, hey, this is what you wanted and you enjoy (most of it), and now you are getting the rewards: more money, more recognition, more opportunities to do what you like, and, hopefully, more time to do them. If you had to do it all over, you would do several things differently, but you learned from the experience, and that makes your value much higher.

This—with variations, depending on the situation, the business, and the individual—is the life of an owner in a start-up.

Your Job as CEO of a Small Business

Being a start-up CEO generally is seen as a glamorous job that is also fun. What it is not seen is the downside of the job with all its frustrations, disillusions, and headaches. So don't be blinded by the luminance of the glamour, but be grounded in the reality of the job that you chose or are thinking of choosing.

Are you in business to have the lifestyle that you always wanted? Is it to make lots of money and become famous? Or is it because you have a vision and want to reach that pinnacle? Whatever your reasons, you have a huge responsibility, because it isn't just you in the limelight; lots of people depend on you being successful.

Aside from you and your family, your employees, your suppliers, and other stakeholders in the business have at least a part of their life tied to you and your company. It is indispensable then that you do your best and become the best owner/CEO that you can be.

Your business should be your passion; if you chose this path is because you enjoy the journey, not just the work. Dropbox co-founder Drew Houston said: "The happiest and most successful people I know don't just love what they do; they are obsessed with solving an important problem, something that matters to them".

While passion is the key ingredient to entrepreneurship, the ability to execute is its married partner. If you cannot deliver, you do not have a business. Before you start a business, you need to know how you will execute and deliver your product or service.

You want to start a business that will be successful; do your homework, validate your idea and ensure that there is a valid market for your product or service. Solve a real problem or offer a significant advantage over existing offerings.

First, you must understand that you not only must assume responsibility for what you do but also for the actions of others, as you are ultimately responsible for everything that happens in your company. The buck stops at your desk.

You must also understand that profits should not be the goal of the company; they should be the reward for managing the core business successfully. While this may sound idealistic, in practice, it should be the rule that runs the business if you are to achieve success.

CEOs, particularly those of small companies, have different leadership and management styles driven by different personalities. Their styles are usually the product of their backgrounds and experiences, both in their personal lives and in the business world. Some are aggressive, and some are quiet and charismatic, but all are driven to a goal and to a vision. However, style is not important; substance is, and the substance of your job (leadership) can be learned. And with everything that is learned, practice makes it perfect.

You start a business because you have a vision, a goal, a place you want to reach, and a company you want to build. You start to implement that vision. You develop a business plan; you study the market and evaluate your product or service against the needs of the market. You were able to find investors, or you decided to fund it yourself. The base is formed—good job. Your visionary stage is completed. Now you have to make it happen.

As an entrepreneur, you started a business and led it through the initial stages and, perhaps, even longer. As the owner/founder, you assumed the position of CEO (or whatever title you chose to use), but carrying the title or the position by default does not necessarily mean you are the right person for it. To confirm yourself as CEO, you need to understand—*really* understand—all the implications and demands of the position, as well as your desires and qualifications.

The two main questions you need to answer are: (1) are you qualified, and (2) do you want to be the CEO? These two questions are independent and unrelated to each other, as qualifications and desire are not mutually exclusive. You may be qualified but prefer to do a different job, or conversely, you may want the position but are not able be the leader the business needs.

Regardless of your title, you are the keeper and driver of the vision, not just for the starting period but forever. However, in starting a business, the vision is not enough to build the company; you have to take command and actually run the start-up and build it into a real company. Your role is now changing into that of a visionary/leader. As a leader, you must attract the right people, and you must lead and keep them motivated.

The same traits that provide founders with a competitive advantage when starting a business also frequently hinder their ability to adapt and flex their style with changing organization demands as the company grows. Their strength of personality frequently impacts those around them more powerfully than they might realize.

As the leader, you must guide your team on the key priorities, set the goals to be achieved, develop the strategies, formulate the action plans, assign duties and responsibilities, and hold people—and yourself—accountable. Developing a strategic plan should be one of the first items on your agenda as the leader. A strategic plan should be the guideline to run the company through the right phases.

Build your team with the best possible members. Do not hesitate to hire people who are smarter than you or know more than you do. The better your team, the better your chances of winning the race to success. Great ideas are important but even more critical is to have the right people in the correct positions to execute them. The more talent on your team, the easier it will be for you to lead.

To build a team that will play as a team—as opposed to a group of individual players—use the terms "we" and "our" when referring to the business. This practice will multiply the talents in the game and lead to a better company. Conversely, selfish owners who only think of "my" company and "my" glory are far less likely to form a real team, and thus, they limit the potential of the company.

As noted by Jack Welch, "Your success as a leader will

come not from what you do every day but from the reflected glory of your team's performance."

You must understand that, while your team may be motivated, no one will have the same drive as you have as the visionary. You will feed their motivation by leading the team to execute the strategic plan and demonstrating that it is the right plan to achieve the vision. Vision was the reason your company was born, but leadership will be the reason it becomes great.

Be eager to learn about everything related to the business. The more you know, the better leader you will be and the higher your chances for success. Also, being an expert will get you recognition, as well as recognition for the business. Don't forget that you are the CEO, so your learning should be directed to leading.

While skills in leadership constitute the efficacy of a leader, character traits determine the quality of the leadership. Your character is important to your job and to your employees. I'm sure you are certain that you have good character, but what's important for this subject is to know what traits are expected in a good leader. You can develop the skills to be a good leader, but it will be much more difficult for you to develop the character needed for optimum leadership.

Abraham Lincoln said, "Nearly all men can stand adversity, but if you want to see a man's character, give him power."

Managing Your Business

More difficult than starting a company is staying in business. You read the statistics earlier in this book, but yet in every corner of the country, you see new stores, restaurants, and shops of all kinds opening up for business. From the statistics, we accept that starting is the easy part, but making it to the desired goal is not so easy.

The following advice is intended—as is the entire book—for small-business start-ups (those ventures started by entrepreneurs who aim to build a business) pulling from the bootstraps and with little or no major investors. Cash is king. Be frugal in managing your money, particularly during the initial stages of the new venture.

As the founder of a new business, you need to be prepared to do all kinds of jobs, from drafting and implementing the business plan to emptying the garbage cans and cleaning the floors. No menial job will take away your position as owner, CEO, president, or whatever other title you choose to give yourself.

Do not add to the payroll more than you absolutely have to. As you build a team, fill all roles based on needed functions, not just titles. Keep the company lean. Use outside services wherever possible instead of adding fixed overhead. Although HR is a critical function, you do not need a full-time person for this job until you reach the size to justify it. There are plenty of independent consultants that serve this purpose for start-ups.

You are the best salesperson to sell your company, so you don't need a PR firm to do the job for you. Identify your company's unique story, and become a raving fan for your business. You are the best keeper of the monetary resources of your company; learn to manage the finances, and hire a part-time bookkeeper to assist you, rather than hiring a highly paid controller or CFO.

Unquestionably, financial management is the most important activity of a start-up (and of every business for that matter). And as such, it should be a main focus of your activities. You do not need to be a financial expert, but you must ensure that finances are well managed and that you thoroughly understand them.

> ***From my experience:*** *I have seen too many business owners who do not give money management the importance it deserves. For example, at least two of my clients used the balance in the checking account as the gage to judge the success of the business. They would typically say "I know I'm doing OK because I have a healthy balance in my checking account". Obviously, this is no way to manage a business. Financial management needs to be the primary concern of all business owners.*

A knowledgeable corporation attorney is needed to help with the legal formation of the enterprise and other legal matters, but you do not need the most expensive law firm in the area. Build a relationship with a competent and experienced attorney who will get to know you and your business intimately and will help you in all future dealings.

The knowledge and experience of your attorney will be demonstrated in drafting the legal documents that administer the life of the company. For example, if you bring in investors, make sure that the legal agreements are drawn with the future of the company and how it will grow in mind.

It is not unusual for new business owners to think in terms of the excitement of the moment and not in the long-term health of the company. An offer to invest can blind an entrepreneur and not let him or her see the effect it can have on future investors and the life of the company.

The attorney will play a key role in drafting the operating agreement (OA) that will rule present and future investments, dilution of original investors, and capitalization of the venture. The OA should not include a no-dilution clause for early or later investors, and the capitalization table must show that all investors get their shares diluted as new investors join.

It is typical of new business owners who have a reasonable amount of money—whether it came from personal funds or investors—to hire employees too soon. If you need help at the beginning, use freelancers you can dismiss quickly if you have to, or use part-timers with a minimum amount of essential hours.

On a separate but somewhat related issue, do not give high titles to people just to be able to convince them to join your company. Giving unjustified titles can create severe problems later on. Creating a vice president role, for example, to hire someone who will not be capable to perform at that level as the company grows will severely limit your options later.

> **From my experience:** *A former client and friend hired a very knowledgeable engineer expert in the core business of the company as a key and almost indispensable member of the startup. To convince him to take the risk of joining a new venture my friend gave him the title of vice president of engineering. As the company grew and became a successful enterprise it became obvious that the engineer did not act or had the capability to operate as a high-level executive.*
>
> *My friend could not release him because his engineering talents were too valuable to give up, but he faced a conundrum to keep him motivated and also build the organization for the long term. Finally, upon my advice, the*

VP title was changed to Chief Technical Officer without any managerial responsibilities. He was happy with his new title and my friend was able to continue to build the organization without the wrongly placed person.

You have several choices when it comes to selling channels. Will you sell direct or through distributors? Will you sell online or through brick-and-mortar facilities? Will you use in-house salespeople or representatives? I favor the use of rep organizations as a more economical and efficient sales channel. However, these organizations must be selected well, incentivized well, and managed properly.[13]

In deciding whether to do something yourself or hire someone to do it, consider your expertise to do it, your preferences, and the costs involved. Are you better off doing this job yourself? Is this what you like to do? Can someone else do it better? Is this the best use of your time? Would you be more efficient doing this or concentrating on your job as the owner?

J. D. Roth in *Entrepreneur* proposes to use a simple calculation to decide if you should spend your time doing these extra jobs, strictly from a cost-of-your-time point of view.[14] He suggests taking your total income from all sources and dividing it by two thousand, the number of hours in a standard work year based on a forty-hour work week. If this hourly wage is greater than the cost to pay somebody else to do the particular job, pay others to do it; if not, do it yourself.

In choosing your personal activities, consider the results of a survey done by the E-Myth organization.[15] It found that business owners who dedicated at least 40 percent of their personal time to marketing and sales grew their revenues 60 percent faster than those who did not. Even more importantly, these companies grew their profits at an even faster rate.

How you split the time between marketing and sales will depend on your individual skills. Unless marketing and sales are your preferred fields, it is typical to feel that you are too busy to dedicate so much time to them, but you must think with your growth mentality and find the right mix for your personal time.

Even if investors are pushing you to spend on employees, facilities, or equipment, do not listen to them if you can go without those expenditures.

From my experience: The startup I joined when I left IBM, was not the typical small business startup that I focus on in this book; rather, it was more like a typical VC-backed large-company candidate startup. It was cash-rich thanks to sizeable investments from VCs who believed in the company, and with a large founding team. Nevertheless, it serves to illustrate my points above.

When I reported to work as a founding member and responsible for a good part of the operations, I was told by the chairman and principal founder that I had x amount of dollars to spend to build the piece of the company under my direction. I told him that I did not need that much and that, as a startup, I thought we needed to be frugal and—for example—we could lease the equipment instead of buying it. I was told that the amount had been reserved for that purpose and thus I should go ahead and spend it.

Spending is easy, so I did that. The same "philosophy" was employed with the rest of the company and, consequently, we drained large amounts of cash. The error of this mandate was experienced when—for a number of reasons that are not relevant here—we exhausted the capital and eventually went into bankruptcy.

Had we been more conscious of expenditures and conserved cash, perhaps we could have avoided the bankruptcy phantom.

The old saying, "If you don't grow you die," should be considered with its hidden significance. Growth at any cost—meaning bulking the top line—can result exactly in that—a heavy cost, such as financial demise. Growth can be achieved in many forms and not necessarily only in size or revenues. A business can grow in technical capabilities, product offerings, market coverage, strengths of the team, and many other ways.

Growing without a unique focus on the top line requires more wisdom, humility, and restraint, recognizing the values inherent in the company and the personal values of the owner. Focusing on customer needs and in creating a strong organization would yield benefits long term. Growth in these areas would prepare the company for steady and vigorous advance, securing loyal customers and the technical viability of the company.

As an entrepreneur and business owner, you are willing (or should be) to invest all your effort, heart, and soul into your company, but you should stop short of investing all your assets. Entrepreneurial focus and dedication are great, but using a retirement account to smooth out uneven cash periods or a home-equity loan during a hard time are actions that you should avoid. Investing and leveraging everything you have to save a business, most of the time, results in failure for the business and pandemonium for the owner.

I am all in favor of avoiding outside investors or partnerships, but destroying your financial security is not a risk worth taking. Before putting extra money into the business, separate an amount that would keep your family safe for a reasonable period until you project recovery of the business.

Not stacking enough cash is probably why the majority of firms go out of business says Bill Klein, president of Consero Global, a financial consulting firm that works with small businesses. Develop close personal relationships with your banker (not just with the bank) from the beginning so you can increase your chances of getting help from the bank when you need it.

Most small-business owners fail to think and plan for tomorrow, assuming that the business will cover any emergency. Retirement plans, college funds, expansion expenses, and other future concerns are not a priority when you are super enthusiastic about your business, but an unexpected quick turn south can find you financially naked and exposed. Be passionate about insulating your family and personal well-being from those risks.

A business owner—primarily a new business owner—must be continuously asking, "What are the main drivers of my business? Where are we now? Where are we going, and where are we going to be in x quarters or years from now?" Also, "What are we doing right, and where can we improve?" The answers to these questions will provide an ongoing real-time picture of the business and ideas to improve it.

The ability to anticipate problems can be an extremely valuable skill of a business owner. There is a technique used by start-ups and even large companies that the *Harvard Business Review* has called a premortem.[16] The technique is intended to anticipate failures.

A pre-mortem is the hypothetical opposite of a postmortem. A pre-mortem in a business setting comes at the beginning of a project rather than the end so that the project can be improved rather than analyzed after it fails. Unlike a typical critiquing session in which team members are asked what *might* go wrong, the pre-mortem operates on the assumption that the project has failed and so asks what *did* go wrong. The team members' task is to generate plausible reasons for the project's failure.

Next to money, perhaps the most important personal asset that you must manage is time. Because there are so many things to do, plan, execute, and think about, there is never enough time. Time is the only thing that we all have the same amount of (twenty-four hours in a day, seven days in a week, etc.). And once we use our time, it is gone. We cannot go to the bank and ask for a loan on time; time is not loaned, and it cannot be replenished.

That is why managing time is so important, and allocating finite amount of time to the innumerable things on your plate is so critical to the success of your business. A survey by the NFIB determined typical ways in which small-business owners use their time:

- 50 percent of them work an average of fifty hours per week, and 48 percent work between fifty and seventy hours per week
- 35 percent believe they misallocate their time and need to do a better job of managing it (my own experience says that a higher number really do a poor job in time management)[17]

We tend to work on what we like to do, regardless of priorities, and we tend to work on the urgent rather than on the important; small-business owners are not exceptions.

- 34 percent like customer service or relations
- 25 percent like producing goods or services
- 37 percent dislike financial issues

- 25 percent dislike employee-related matters (my own experience says a much higher percentage dislike all employee-related issues)

How small-business owners spend most of their time:

- 27 percent producing goods and services
- 25 percent serving customers
- 13 percent in marketing and sales
- 11 percent in financial issues
- 10 percent planning and strategizing
- 4 percent in employee-related matters
- 3 percent learning and gathering information
- 1 percent in administration
- 6 percent in other areas

As the company grows, these numbers should (and will) change as the owner will (and should) become less involved in the doing to concentrate more on the planning and strategizing. In other words, this will be a transition from the technician state to the manager state to the CEO state.

Building a team is an essential part of the CEO job. Having a competitive team is a major component for profitability, cash flow, and the owner's personal satisfaction. Liz Wiseman highlights the importance of team building, suggesting that leaders (whom she calls "multipliers") get so much from their people that they effectively double the workforce at no additional cost.[18] Micromanagers, on the other hand, underutilize talent and resources.

The SOHO report mentioned earlier identified hiring decisions as the best and worst decisions of business owners. This emanates from the quality of the team formed or being formed and its ability to be a growth team. Selecting, hiring, and motivating employees are principal components of success.

The excitement of starting to form an organization may drive you to rush some decisions in hiring. It is exhilarating to fill that first slot and get things rolling, but the wrong decision here can multiply through successive hires. A large company can make several mistakes in hiring without seriously affecting its wellbeing, but a new or small company can be seriously damaged by just one wrong hire. You want to create a good culture in your organization and it must start with the first hire.

Your first employee is a huge financial investment in your new journey, so you need to understand how this employee will contribute to your bottom line or otherwise to the growth of the company. Make sure you have a definite role to fill and not just a vague position. Define the job with a thorough job description and use a functional organization chart to identify the needs of the business.

A functional organization chart is designed to identify all functions needed to carry out the business of the company. It is a dynamic document that grows as the need of the company grows and new functions are defined. Hiring should strictly follow the need to fill those functions. Exceptions should only be to secure a star employee who will be instrumental later in the growth of the business.

The job interview to select candidates is the main part of the hiring process. The quality of the interview can determine the quality of selected candidates. Unfortunately, many managers (including business owners) are not knowledgeable in interviewing. *Fundamentals of Job Interviewing for Managers* provides directions and suggestions for an effective interview.[22]

Also pertinent to the growth of the company is the requirement for systems and procedures. The E-Myth tells us about the need to think about systems, not people, saying that a company must be run by systems, as in a franchise. If you want your business to provide consistent and predictable results, you need to create the franchise model.

Consistency in management and in operations is critical to growing a business and to freeing the entrepreneur/owner to lead. If no aspect of a business is left to chance, the owner's ability to achieve the business and personal goals are greatly enhanced. Also enhanced is the owner's ability to free him or herself from the daily grind of the business.

Documenting all processes and procedures in a good operations manual will provide consistency in operations and in the value to your customers and other stakeholders. This document is more than a static text; it is the bible of the business. It is the guarantee that this is the way we do it here to ensure the quality of products and services that will guide you to a successful end.

Many (most?) small-business owners postpone the development of systems, believing that it is not a requirement for their budding company, and they fail to recognize the advantage of having valuable systems in place. However, it is much easier and efficient to develop and implement systems when the company is small, rather than doing it when the size of the company makes it more complicated. Let the systems grow with the company, and you will reap the rewards.

The path to growth that a new (or any) business must follow depends on the creation of the right behaviors in the owner and in the team. Creating a culture of empowerment and accountability within the general culture of the company will drive the business down the right path.[19,20]

John D. Rockefeller identified three underlying habits as key to the successful management of a business. The three fundamental barriers to growth that he identified—and the trio of "Rockefeller habits"[21] that he developed to cope with those barriers—haven't changed in their importance since they were first published.

The Three Barriers

- Leadership: Can the leadership team keep growing in its ability to delegate and predict the course of the business? Can it develop other leaders?

- Systems and structures: Will the support and operational systems be installed to help drive timely decision making? Will organizational structures be set up to keep clear who is accountable?

- Market dynamics: Will the organization be prepared to deal with the changing competitive and economic pressures that come with growth? Will the organization recognize when it must shift its economic model?

The Three Rockefeller Habits

- Priorities: Does the company have five top priorities for the year and the quarter and a clear number-one

- Priority, along with an appropriate theme? Do everyone's personal priorities align with the company's?

- Data: Does the business have sufficient data on a regular basis to provide insight into how well it is running? Does everyone have at least one key daily or weekly metric driving his or her performance?

- Rhythm: Does the organization have an effective rhythm of daily, weekly, monthly, quarterly, and annual meetings to maintain alignment and drive accountability? Are the meetings well run and useful?

As Thomas Edison said, "Opportunity is missed by most people because it is dressed in overalls and looks like work." Take advantage of all opportunities offered to you that are in line with your goals and your business model.

Chapter VI – Winning the Game

Survival of Businesses

As discussed earlier, according to *Small Business Administration* research, only half of new businesses survive for the first five years, and only one-third of new businesses are able to survive for ten years. The inverse is compelling as we can conclude that if only 50 percent of new businesses survive for the first five years, then the other 50 percent fail in the first five years and that about 65 percent of new businesses don't make it to the ten-year mark. Forbes reports an even grimmer statistic based on Bloomberg research: eight of every ten businesses fail within the first eighteen months.

Further statistics indicate that about 10 to 12 percent of firms with employees open each year, and about 10 to 12 percent close. Firms without employees (solo owner) have turnover rates three times as high as employer firms, mostly because it is easier for solo entrepreneurs to start and stop, as they tend to be smaller than firms that employ others.

The reasons businesses fail are as many and as varied as the type of businesses.

- Leadership failure: Dysfunctional leadership will affect the entire company. Lack of leadership can reflect in many ways, from financial management to employee relations. A business without a leader is like a ship without a helmsman.
- Insufficient resources: Whether financial, technical, personnel, or otherwise, not having the required resources can kill a business.

- Unprofitable business model: Just having a killer idea is not enough; a business needs the right plan and the right execution to succeed.
- Lack of adequate planning: Business, sales, marketing, operations, and employment plans can be summarized into a strategic plan, which is the lifeblood of the business.
- Not in touch with customers or do not understand their needs or desires: This is part of the marketing/sales plan and a prerequisite to survival.
- Lack of a unique differentiation and value: Your idea is great, but how is it different from what is already available, and how different is your approach to the market?
- Poor financial management: Cash is king, and not managing the financial pieces right means catastrophe.
- Failure to communicate the unique value proposition: If you have a unique value but fail to communicate it, you may as well not have one.
- Failure to achieve market fit for the product or service: Your products or services must be in demand, and your offerings must match that demand.
- Bad execution of a plan: Planning is key, but without execution, no plan is valid. The plan must include rules for its execution and accountability at all levels.
- Rapid growth and overexpansion: This is a typical mistake many businesses make. Overenthusiastic about the success achieved, they embark on an aggressive expansion that exceeds the resources available.

Business Failures by Entrepreneurial Mistakes

Obviously and sadly, many business failures are due to mistakes that the owners make, mostly for lack of experience and/or being naïve in the business world. Some typical mistakes are [22].

- assuming that your idea is unique and a winner
  - They don't know their key competitors and their strength.
  - They don't know if there is a substitute for their idea.
  - They don't know how the need for their idea is met today.
- lack of objectivity
  - They are the only ones offering feedback for their idea.
  - They can't name the negatives or cons of their idea.
- failure to plan
  - Their plan is only in their head
  - They don't believe in planning or claim they don't have time for it
- fear of failure
  - They cannot see the positive in what is happening.
  - Their time is spent worrying and not in proactively advancing the goal.
- underestimating the resources needed
  - They fail to implement milestones for the completion of projects or evaluate progress.
  - They fail to consider contingency factors.
- failure to delegate

- They believe they are the only ones who can do the job.
- All assignments require their approval.
- trying to compete in price
  - They believe that customers only care about price.
  - They cannot state the difference between their business and others'.
- they fail to think outside the box
  - Their vision is fragmented and not part of an integrated whole.
  - Their vision is stuck in the present and with an uncertain future.
- failure to recognize the value of good employees
  - They do not provide motivation for employees to excel.
  - They do not have a process for selecting the best employees.
- failure to recognize what builds business value
  - They believe value is only measured by sales and profits.
  - They believe they are the primary element that causes the business to be successful.[23]

Giving customers what they want is a prerequisite for success. In a recent interview with *Inc.500*, Paul Graham rightly claimed that many times, start-ups fail for the same reason restaurants do, such as bad food. He illustrated this claim by saying that if the food is good, the restaurant can be in an unattractive and out-of-the-way location, be expensive and have poor service, but people will still go there.

However, if it has bad food, a beautiful location and lots of shiny stuff will not attract clients. The same is true for any business; it must offer what people want, and if the business fails it is because it did not cater to clients' needs.

Starting a business is an exciting endeavor that requires having a clearly identified market demand for the product or service that is the basis for the business. Success depends on careful strategic planning and sound fiscal management that begin prior to start-up and continue throughout the life of the business.

Execution of the plan is what drives results. A beautiful plan not implemented with equally good execution does nothing for a successful business. This execution gap is a breach between the company's strategy and expectation and its ability to meet the goals and put ideas into action.

Kaplan and Norton claim that fewer than 10 percent of well-formulated strategies are successfully implemented.[23] Some of the reasons are:

- The strategy is not clear and/or not grounded in reality. Goals should be realistic and following the SMART concept (Strategic, Measurable, Attainable, Realistic, Timely.)
- The strategy is not communicated well, and buy-in by employees is not reached. Clear and concise communication is essential for employees to understand what is expected of them. Not knowing the way will feed disappointment and unhappiness. Employees need to know the what and why of their job.
- The plan does not include employees' participation, and their contributions are not highlighted, and thus, employees are not engaged.
- Execution is not aligned throughout all phases of the company. Many feel isolated or not an integral part of the plan, and everyone goes their own way.
- Employees are not given the resources and support to be—and feel—an important part of the plan.

By their nature, business owners are explorers and curious when it comes to business opportunities, but these traits normally considered good can be distractions that can damage the business. Businesses that don't stay focused on what they are best at end up being beaten by their competitors. Or, as Jim Collins says, more companies die of indigestion (not staying focused on what makes them great) than from starvation (not having opportunities within their focus).

The owner and the leadership team must be crystal clear on the business's focus and make sure they are not distracted off their path by the shiny opportunities they see. It is the owner's responsibility to create a culture of responsibility by monitoring progress and holding people accountable.

The leader must listen (and really hear) team members and accept feedback. He or she must be open to change the course if the situation demands it and, when reaching success, celebrate and share credit with all participants.

> ***From my experience:*** *I coached for years an otherwise brilliant client who "saw opportunities around every corner" and had a tendency to go after all of them. The effect on his business was detrimental because he would constantly take his focus away from the ongoing business to attempt to pursue those shiny opportunities. It took my persistent prodding to get him to refocus on the business at hand and the strategic plan we had developed.*
>
> *Another former client was an inventor who kept changing his focus and the focus of the business according to his latest invention. The result was a business being run as a hobby shop and not the excellent manufacturing company it was supposed to be. The good news is that we both realized that his happiness*

was in the inventing part and thus we changed the strategy of the business making it a specialized shop. The business thrived under this new strategy and the owner was very happy.

Profitability vs. Effort

Typically, in a start-up mode, it is extremely difficult for a business owner to say no to business opportunities. Although getting clients is of paramount importance to a new venture, the owner must use judgment in the selection of clients. In an effort to gain more clients, some business owners don't stop to think whether jobs are profitable, rewarding, and deserving of the time they consume.

Working with projects that cannot deliver healthy profits can sap time and limit growth. Dedicating disproportional time to clients that require much effort will not leave enough time and energy to serve other, more profitable accounts.

Yet, for varied reasons, small businesses sometimes tend to dedicate more effort to accounts that do not deserve it from a profitability standpoint. They do this because of loyalty to some customers for a variety of reasons, such as relationships, personal history, fear of not getting enough clients, and so on.

Conversely, perhaps they do not dedicate sufficient effort to other accounts that should be higher priority. This neglect may be due to perceived value of the account, differences in personalities, lack of history with the customer, and so on.

This imbalance may lead to lower revenues or, worse yet, lower profits. It is important then to find a balance between the efforts that each account deserves and the effort dedicated to them. It follows then that to determine which clients are more valuable, you must score them not just on profits but on profits per effort.

One key issue for any business is to be able to fire customers when they are not worth the effort necessary to serve them. This is a very difficult decision for any business owner but one that must be learned in order to maximize profits.

"What is measured can be managed" is an old truism in business. Following this axiom, one can estimate the effort that each major account deserves. Furthermore, the same approach can be applied to products and services, such as which are in most demand, and which demands the most effort? Which are most profitable relative to the effort necessary to maximize the profits?

In both cases—customers and products or services—look for that sweet spot where loyalty, demand, and profitability intersect, and plan accordingly.

The key for small businesses is not always to think big at the start; it is to focus on a strategy and seek out new opportunities that are truly worthy of their time.

Conclusion

Starting a business is an exciting and rewarding experience. It can offer many advantages, such as the feeling of independence of being your own boss, working on your own schedule, the potential for high earnings, and making a living doing something that you like. However, it can also be an incredibly challenging undertaking that not many people are prepared to grapple with or qualified to lead.

Entrepreneurs face challenges from the time they get up in the morning and throughout the day. Whether they are dealing with investors, trying to solve production problems, dealing with difficult customers, covering payroll, managing people-related issues, or suffering through low sales, their life is a continuous struggle.

In addition to having the proper resources, ideas, products or services, support, and drive, the entrepreneur must have the personality traits that make him or her succeed. Just to be an expert in a particular subject or technology doesn't qualify a person as a potential entrepreneur. It is a small minority of the population that has the suitable personality and stand out as being well suited for dealing with the challenges of the job.

The ability to not only survive the challenges but to use them as learning opportunities and emerge from them stronger and more successful is a unique quality of entrepreneurs. Start-ups are inherently chaotic, and thus, becoming an entrepreneur requires thorough planning, creativity, and a very large dose of hard work.

Andy Grove, former Intel CEO, said, of companies, something that can be translated to people: "Bad companies are destroyed by crisis, good companies survive them, and great companies are improved by them." Similarly, an entrepreneur without the right personality can be overwhelmed by obstacles, good entrepreneurs can survive them, but the sign of a successful entrepreneur is one who emerges as a better leader after facing serious obstacles.

OK, so you decided you have the right personality traits and all the other requirements to be an entrepreneur, but there is another important question to ask: why do you want to do it? Why do you want to start your own business? Is your goal the freedom of the adventure? Is it the pride that comes with it? Is it the hope of making lots of money or becoming famous?

Is it to take a new direction and move into something different and positive, or is it to steer away from what you don't like? Carefully analyze this question, because doing it as a defensive ploy to get away from a bad situation may not be the motivation that you need to succeed. Conversely, a vision of a great business and experience will drive you to success.

Chances are that, at one time, you had a great idea that you believed could be transformed into a million-dollar business (or much more), but the critical part is deciding if this idea can be implemented in practice into a viable business. The answer to this is most likely inherent in the following questions:

- Does your idea have market value?
- Can the concept be executed effectively and efficiently?
- Is your business model profitable?

If you can answer positively to these questions, you have a good chance to make it in the business world.

Next you must develop a good business plan. This has to be a realistic plan, not a pie-in-the-sky plan to feed your optimism and make you feel good about your idea. You cannot do this plan in an abstract way; you must do the necessary research to base your assumptions in valid data. And do not forget to prepare for unexpected drawbacks and include a plan B and even a plan C in case things don't go according to the main strategy.

Do not do the plan in isolation; consult with people or organizations that can provide valuable data and support to ensure its viability. This will be your road to success, and as such, it must be as realistic as possible. It must also be dynamic, because you must adjust it as you learn new information that can affect the outcome.

Regardless of how good the plan is, the key will be in its execution. A beautiful plan with bad execution will not take you to where you want to go. Choosing the correct path is crucial, but equally vital is choosing the right vehicle to carry you, and that vehicle is the good execution of the appropriate plan.

You do not know it all; in fact, you do not know what you do not know. So do not make the mistake of trying to do it all alone; get support from others, particularly from someone who has done it before, a coach, or a business support group. An experienced business coach can make the experience a much easier one, but make sure it is someone who you can work with and who understands your vision and personality.

Joining a peer-advisory board will give you the double benefit of a coach and a support group composed of other business owners. This, in fact, acts as your own board to guide you through all the business issues and also deal with some personal issues that may affect the business. (See the appendix.)

If you made the decision and started the journey, congratulations; you are joining a select group of people who are important contributors to society. Your vision is the goal, and your talent, perseverance, creativity, and hard work are the motivators to lead you to the goal.

But to complete your happiness, remember what I said earlier in this book:

A business should be a part of your life, apart from your life, and should not be your entire life.

Meaning that your personal and family life must be preserved during the challenging times of starting and running a business. You must sacrifice many things to become a business owner, but to ensure happiness, your personal and family life should not be among the things that you sacrifice.

Now that you finished reading this book and had a chance to think about the joys and perils of business ownership, let me repeat the question I asked in the introduction:

Are you ready to mount the lion and survive?

If your answer is affirmative, I congratulate you and wish you much success and happiness doing what you like to do.

.

Appendix

The Role of Boards of Directors in Small Companies
(previously published by Oswald R. Viva in 2001)

Importance of a Board

Boards of directors are common among high-tech start-ups and fast-growing companies and are mandatory for public companies. They are, typically, key contributors to the success of those companies. Most boards of directors are composed of experienced businesspersons, investors, and others who can provide expertise in the direction of the venture. They yield sufficient power to replace the management team if they consider the performance to be less than acceptable.

Commonly, they receive monetary compensation and, in many cases, equity participation as well. Being responsible for the business, board members are exposed to personal liability, thus, forcing the company to provide costly directors and officers' liability insurance coverage.

Boards of directors exist to hold management accountable for achieving the business plan, creating shareholder value, and assisting the owner/CEO in growing the enterprise. They also provide advice and counsel, but their primary function is to ensure accountability. A strong board can also help a young company build credibility in the outside world.

Most owners of small or midsize businesses perceive the

keys to success and long-term growth to be new products, new markets, and solid management. Most small businesses don't have a board of directors because they cannot afford one and because their owners don't think they need one.

In fact, the perception of most small-business owners is that a board of directors is only for big businesses. This cannot be further from the truth, though, as most entrepreneurs desperately need a source of advice and support and the accountability of having to report to someone.

Accountability is a key to the success of entrepreneurial ventures. Business owners love the fact that they report to no one; as owners, they have the God-given right to procrastinate, and consciously or unconsciously, this is one of the major driving factors for many people becoming business owners.

The flip side, however, is a lack of accountability that too often leads them to complacency and failure. As entrepreneurs, they get too involved in the day-to-day running of the business, in firefighting, and in doing the things they like or feel comfortable doing while neglecting the leadership activities, and eventually they lose sight of their driving vision. The end result is that the business doesn't evolve, and owners eventually find running the company increasingly unpleasant or beyond their capabilities.

For private companies, putting together a board with outside directors is optional, but there are undisputable reasons to have one. Assembling a team of diverse, active directors sets a course for long-term stability of the company, and having that external source of accountability is key for keeping companies, and particularly privately owned businesses, moving forward.

The reality is, however, that most small businesses cannot afford a costly board of directors, and thus, they must find other effective ways to get the accountability and help they need.

Advisory Boards

An advisory board is a viable alternative. "Companies can get tremendous benefit from thinking outside the box; this may mean approaching business executives in very different industries or someone who sees the world of business from a very different perspective," advises Jeff Simmons, a partner at Raphael and Raphael, a Boston accounting firm. Setting up a team of advisers can provide the entrepreneurs with valuable outside guidance.

The entrepreneur who starts a business on a great idea but has no managerial experience can be lost in the hard world of business. Seasoned entrepreneurial executives who have been through it all before can guide them and help them avoid pitfalls. It is a fact that very few entrepreneurs have all the skills needed in running a business.

It's rare for someone to understand administration, operations, finance, sales and marketing, and human resources and to be a great leader as well. So it makes sense to find board members who can complement the skills of the entrepreneur.

For many start-up companies, the board ends up being the founders of the company and, perhaps, the accountant, attorney, family, and friends. However, there is huge value in expanding the board to include outside directors—those who do not work for the company and are not family or friends but offer their time and advice to help shape and guide the company. There is a price to pay for these benefits, as the founders give up some control when they put outsiders on the board.

A board of peers relieves the feeling of being lonely at the top that most owners and leaders of small enterprises have.

Entrepreneurs need a forum where they can openly express their ideas, concerns, and plans. In every company, there are many issues that the CEO cannot openly discuss with employees, i.e., plans that affect those inside the company, but an outside board gives him a valuable sounding board where he can openly and candidly talk about them.

Selecting Members

Once the purpose of the board is clearly defined, the CEO must dedicate the effort to recruit the right board members. They must be the best people available who fit the purpose; they must have the expertise to help in the management of the company and a shared understanding of what the mission and needs of the company are. An effective board is composed of outsiders who have been through the entrepreneurial process and understand the operating issues that a growth-oriented company typically faces.

If the advisory boards are composed of CPAs, attorneys, and other professionals who work for the company in their profession, the board may fail. It is difficult for them to give disinterested opinions because they are paid by the business, and they don't want to lose it as a client. Also, having a bunch of yes-men or women in a board may be good for the ego of the owner/CEO, but they will not contribute with innovative ideas or harsh criticism sometimes needed.

It is important to recruit board members who have similar values to those of the CEO so that the board will not be a mismatch with the culture created by the owner/CEO. He or she must be clear about the expectations and must make sure the potential board members agree with them. Personal chemistry does matter; it makes sense to take the time to find qualified outsiders who have a good rapport with the company's leadership and an informed interest in the industry's challenges.

It is clear that having a board of directors or advisers can be very useful to the entrepreneurial CEO, however, it is not a question of forming or joining a board and expecting results automatically. He or she must be willing and able to be completely open and truthful and to dedicate effort and time to the board and its directives or advice. Communication with the board must be frequent, candid, and complete about all aspects of the business, good or bad. The board cannot help the CEO develop strategies or solve problems if it doesn't know what's going on.

What Type of Board?

What is the right type of board for a small company? Can the company afford a highly paid board of outside experts? Is the CEO/entrepreneur ready to report to a body of outsiders? Can he or she interface openly and humbly with them? Can he or she accept that a group of outsiders, who previously had no role in the company, will tell him or her what to do? After all, he or she is the one who put all the sweat and tears in forming, growing, and managing the company. Is an advisory board or a managing board best suited for the situation?

These are choices that the CEO must make to select the best alternative for the business. The decision on whether to have a board with outside directors should be based on an understanding of the value expected from the board, the needs of the company, and the needs of the CEO/entrepreneur. A board of directors that is formed without well-defined purposes or with the wrong expectations is doomed to fail.

The most common type of boards is paid boards with outside directors who meet to monitor the progress of the company. If everything is going well, they tend not to have much to say. If there are problems or issues, they are often critical of the CEO and the management team and can take action of some sort. A board can also meet more frequently and offer significant ongoing support and help the owner or management team in the strategic decisions affecting the company.

The working board brings the CEO into regular contact with knowledgeable people whose wide experience can prove enormously helpful. The working board also helps the CEO fight the isolation that comes with leadership, no matter what the size of the company. Since management must report to the board regarding all aspects of the business, the working board brings a helpful discipline to the operations of a closely held firm.

The board also can help resolve family issues surrounding the small or midsize firm, particularly when management must deal with disgruntled family members. Another tangible advantage is that a board gives the firm visibility in the outside world, connecting it with financing sources, acquisition targets, strategic partnership opportunities, and the community in general.

Nevertheless, paid boards also have significant disadvantages. In addition to the high cost and the issues already discussed, some entrepreneurs don't want to spend time recruiting members, planning agendas, and luring advisers to meetings. Not every CEO of privately held corporations is fond of independent boards of directors because, by definition, the working board strips the CEO of his or her autonomy, and for many CEOs, that's a good reason not to have one.

Many privately held companies are opting instead for informal advisory boards. As elected members, directors have a fiduciary duty to the shareholders and to the corporation and are potential targets of lawsuit; consequently, they must be insured by the corporation with directors and officers (D&O) liability insurance.

Advisers don't face the same risks; as a result, a very viable alternative that is becoming very popular is for busy entrepreneurs to turn to peer-advisory groups in which local businesspeople meet regularly with a facilitator and help one another solve problems.

Alternative Boards

In their best form, these alternative boards are created and facilitated by specialized organizations that have developed systems proven in the multiplicity of boards formed within them and improved with the experience generated in the large number of boards managed. The system relies on the combined experience of the members in their various fields, bringing to the table a wide range of expertise.

They offer small and midsize business owners independent views that are based on a variety of approaches to the solution of problems. They also act as sounding boards and infuse each member with valuable new ideas. One of the key advantages of these alternative boards over the paid boards is their much lower cost and the absence of liability of the members.

The two most significant of these organizations are The Alternative Board, or TAB, (www.TABboards.com) in Denver, Colorado, and Vistage (www.vistage.com) in San Diego, California. Two elements that make these systems work are the commitment of members and an experienced, trained facilitator. Membership is by invitation only, based on each candidate's qualifications.

The facilitator confers with each member prior to the monthly group meetings and identifies issues to be placed on the agenda for a timely discussion. These standards result in compatible and committed groups; members typically stay in the system many years.

The boards are composed of owners and leaders of noncompeting businesses of similar size. They meet monthly to discuss problems and opportunities in a relaxed and confidential atmosphere. Members are matched according to business size, type, and complexity; experience; and even personalities. Each board usually has members operating businesses in different industries. This diversity of backgrounds provides a cross-fertilization of ideas that are not locked in the thinking of any one industry.

Perspective may be one of the most important business assets money can't buy, but the approach of these alternative boards provides fresh ideas and vision from different perspectives. By adding the dimension of the monthly meeting and a coach/facilitator who they meet with every month, the system adds continuity and consistency in the reporting and exchange of ideas.

At the meetings, owners discuss issues of common interest, problems, concerns, and opportunities of each member. The meetings are chaired by a facilitator trained in the system, who him or herself is a business expert with many years of management experience. In fact, between members and facilitator, a typical peer-advisory board has between two hundred and three hundred years of combined management experience.

At the board meetings, business owners receive advice and

support but also the accountability so badly needed. The accountability and advice are more valuable because they come from fellow successful business owners who most likely have faced or will face similar problems or issues. The dynamics of the meeting keeps the participants moving in the right direction, because all the business owners in the group understand each other's formulas for success and what the individual and collective needs are.

One of the keys is that each member shares his or her company strategy and action plan, as well as his or her personal visions and missions. It is the strategic vision that is so difficult to maintain when you're spending all your energy making the business work from one day to the next.

Consequently, one of the priorities of these boards is the guidance provided by the facilitator to develop the vision, mission, and strategic planning of each of the member companies. The plans are reviewed by the boards and followed throughout the implementation of the strategies and tactics.

Steve Scharr, president of Metal Sales & Service, a manufacturer of metal ornamental structures in Kenneth Square, Pennsylvania, says, "I know that I need to work on strategic planning, but it seems that I always have some fires to put out that are more urgent than the planning, but the peer pressure of my board and the guidance of the facilitator help me to get off center and work on much-needed strategies."

He continues, "In a recent meeting, we reviewed our budgets for the year, comparing them to benchmarks for our businesses. We all learned from the process, and we feel better about our ability to plan and budget." Steve is referring to his board of directors, a TAB board he joined together with five other leaders of noncompeting businesses.

Even companies that have their own board of directors find having access to a group of peers is invaluable, according to Charles Boisseau in "Peer Pressure for Entrepreneurs" at LocalBusiness.com. He quotes Jewell Esposito (CEO and founder of 2e Corporation, a fourteen-month-old Sterling, Virginia-based company), who said the four outside directors on her board are helpful in providing contacts in the industry, such as venture capitalists, but they can't help with sticky day-to-day issues of running her eleven-employee company.

So she joined a board that has several women among its members. Esposito said that this board provides her support and insight from other women business owners she cannot receive from her formal board. Just as important, she said, is that the group provides her a regular outlet to think longer term about her business. "They remind me to keep my role as the visionary of the company," she said.

The key to success is the willingness of the participating business owners to expose the details of their companies to the group, under the protection of confidentiality. Since only noncompeting businesses are allowed in the same group, members talk about touchy issues, such as selling a business or firing an employee, that they may not be able to discuss with their employees. "It's a no-holds-barred environment."

As John Chapin III (president of Power Modules, Inc., a distributor of specialized heating elements in Norristown, Pennsylvania) says, "I am a member of TAB because I like having my own kitchen cabinet that will tell me what they think rather than what I want to hear. It's the only group I can answer honestly when I'm asked, 'How's business?' If I do something that is not the right way, they let me know in no uncertain terms," he says.

Notes

1. TTI Performance Systems Ltd., Scottsdale, AZ.

2. Jessica Bruder, "The Psychological Price of Entrepreneurship", Inc Magazine, September 2013.

3. "A Visual Entrepreneurial Blog," Entrepreneur magazine, September 3, 2013.

4. Funders and Founders blog, www.foundersandfounders.com

5. Target Training International Ltd., Scottsdale, AZ

6. Michael Berger, "The E-Myth Revisited", HarperCollins Publishers, Inc. 1999.

7. Shore Consulting blogging, www.jeffshore.com.

8. Survey of Inc.500 Companies, Inc Magazine, September 2013.

9. Oswald R. Viva, "It's Lonely at the Top: A Practical Guide to Become a Better Leader for Your Small Company", iUniverse 2011.

10. Ben Horowitz; Ben's Blog, www.bhorowitz.com, August 13, 2013.

11. John F. Dini, "Hunting in a Farmer's World: Celebrating the Mind of an Entrepreneur", Gardendale Press, 2014.

12. Ralph Waldo Emerson Quotes, Brainy Quotes, www.brainyquote.com.

13. Oswald R. Viva, "Sales Reps as Successful Sales Channels for Small Businesses," January 2009.

14. J. D. Roth, "Don't Waste Your Time," Entrepreneur magazine, June 2014.

15. "The SOHO Report", Ashland, OR: E-Myth organization, 2014.

16. Gary Klein, "Performing a Project Premortem," Harvard Business Review, 2007.

17. Source NFIB National Small Business Poll, 2012, as published in My Business.

18. Liz Wiseman, "Multipliers: How the Best Leaders Make Everyone Smarter", June 15, 2010.

19. Oswald R. Viva. "Create a Culture of Empowerment", e-book, SkillBites.net, 2012.

20. Oswald R. Viva. "Accountability in the Workplace", e-book, SkillBites.net, 2012.

21. Verne Harnish, "Mastering the Rockefeller Habits: What You Must Do to Increase the Value of Your Growing Firm," March 1, 2011.

22. Brian Nelson, "Ten Mistakes Entrepreneurs Commonly Make" presentation, 2012.

23. Robert Kaplan and David Norton, "The Balanced Scorecard, Translating Strategy Into Action", September 1996.

About the Author

Oswald R. Viva is the founder and president of V&A Management, LLC, a consulting company founded in 1985 and now dedicated to helping small and midsize businesses. He has over twenty years of experience in top corporate management in large and small companies, including multiple C-level positions, fifteen years as consultant in high-tech and manufacturing industries worldwide, and eleven years as CEO and executive coach for small and midsize businesses.

Oswald participated in eight start-ups, either as a principal and founder or as a consultant in an acting leadership position, including holding multiple CEO positions. He was also the owner of one of the most successful franchises of The Alternative Board (TAB). He has served on the board of directors of eight entrepreneurial companies in various fields.

He is the author of several books and e-books, including *It's Lonely at the Top: A Practical Guide to Becoming a Better Leader of Your Small Company*, published by iUniversal in September 2011. He is an occasional speaker in subjects related to business ownership and management and has been a guest on a number of radio programs.

His education includes degrees in mechanical engineering and extensive training in business administration, finance, and management. He is a certified management consultant, coach, and facilitator; a member of the National Federation of Independent Businesses; and a member of the Fortune Business Leaders council. He is the inventor of record for several patents and has received numerous awards in the management and entrepreneurial field.

Born in Argentina, he migrated to the United States fifty-six years ago. He has been married to the love of his life for fifty-six years and resides in Acworth, Georgia. He is the father of four and grandfather of twelve.

www.ingramcontent.com/pod-product-compliance
Lightning Source LLC
Chambersburg PA
CBHW051324170526
45166CB00002B/669